TRAWLIN

with the

LID OFF

To Rosemary with love & kind Regards
John Nicklin   1 September 1996

JOHN NICKLIN

AURORA
PUBLISHING

© This edition AURORA PUBLISHING

ISBN: 1 85926 77 2

Distributed by: **Aurora Enterprises Ltd.**
Unit 9, Bradley Fold Trading Estate,
Radcliffe Moor Road,
Bradley Fold,
BOLTON BL2 6RT
Tel: 01204 370753/2
Fax: 01204 370751

Written by: © **John Nicklin, 1996**

Printed
and bound by: **MFP Design & Print**
Unit E3, Longford Trading Estate,
Thomas Street,
Stretford,
Manchester M32 0JT.

Front cover photograph by John Worthington.

The Author wishes to acknowledge the help given by Mrs. Janet Tierney, curator of Welholme Gallery, Mr Arthur Credland, curator of Hull Docks Museum, and Mr. Agust Georgsson, curator of the Maritime Museum of Iceland in tracing relevant photographs.

***Mr. Sigurgeir Jonasson**, the well known photographer, of Vestmannaeyjar, Iceland for kindly providing photos of Surtsey.*

*The long suffering staff at **Grimsby Central Library**, whose extensive facilities, and patient assistance has been invaluable.*

The Grimsby Evening Telegraph *and* **Hull Daily Mail (Northcliffe Newspaper Group)** *for permission to use photographs from their archives.*

*All of the many ex-colleagues and their next of kin, especially **Skipper Jimmy Williams**, of Hull, who sent me photos; all those men I swilled about the deck with over the years, without whom there would have been nothing to write about; and my publishers, who knocked the script into a state fit to go to the printers.*

*Finally, special thanks to **John Worthington** of Fleetwood for kindly supplying the excellent cover photograph.*

I am grateful to all of you.

John Nicklin

This book is dedicated to the men who manned the distant water trawler fleet, an endangered species now almost extinct.

Exploited throughout their working lives by many unscrupulous shipowners; the bookmakers and publicans who lined their pockets and waxed fat at their expense; and those ladies of the night who patrol the waterfront of every dockyard area on the planet, and whose dubious perfumed charms endeavour to coax the last few shillings out of almost empty pockets; these 'two day millionaires' were finally cast on the scrap heap when a combination of extended fishing limits, and political decisions taken far away from the turbulent waters of the Arctic fishing grounds, which sounded the death knell of the British distant water trawler.

Even in redundancy these men received a poor deal.

After the debacle of the Icelandic Cod Wars the demise of the deep water trawlers was foreseeable and inevitable. The trawler owners realized this and it is a significant fact that very few, if any, new distant water trawlers were built after the end of the cod wars. When the final decommissioning of the trawlers took place most of them were in the last stages of their useful life, and were just one step from the knacker's yard. As a tribute to the power of their influence in the corridors of Whitehall the owners received generous decommissioning grants. After this money was safely tucked away in the bank those ships with any life in them were sold to fish under a foreign flag, or used as a cheap method of providing standby/rescue vessels for the British sector of the North Sea oil fields, or as makeshift marine survey vessels. A double pay off. From this bonanza the men that had previously manned the ships received precisely nothing.

Redundancy pay? "No way," said the owners, "The Redundancy Act does not apply to casual workers."

The few trawlermen that queried this statement at the offices of the Department of Employment were given the same story. This gloomy news was quickly circulated, as bad news will circulate in any close knit community, and the approaches to the Department of Employment ceased.

How men that have worked for the same employer for over thirty years, in some cases spending four or five years on the same ship, can be defined as casual workers defies any rational explanation. A few years later, a crew member of one of the last Hull trawlers to be laid up, challenged the owners' definition of 'casual worker' at an Industrial Tribunal and the Tribunal eventually found in the man's favour. A long procession of appeals and lobbying followed until at last, in 1994, the government was compelled to accept that the trawlermen were entitled to redundancy pay. The award was the minimum possible under the employment legislation and the qualifying conditions were such that most of the men received only a pittance, and a great many were excluded altogether. A fight for a proper redundancy deal is continuing.

When the war clouds finally broke in 1939 the trawlermen from Hull, Grimsby, Fleetwood, Aberdeen and other fishing ports flocked by the thousand to answer the call. A few weeks training at the Sparrows Nest, Lowestoft, and they were on active service. Men wise in the ways of the sea in all its moods, they formed the backbone of the Royal Naval Patrol Service, Harry Tate's navy, and their experience and know how formed a protective cushion for the thousands of their young countrymen that were to join them. Teachers, chemists, bank clerks, carpenters, men deserting the dole queues; men drawn into a foreign, hostile environment by the demands of war, they were nursed through the critical early days by the nucleus of trawlermen that, whether by accident or design, crewed the mine sweepers, armed trawlers and corvettes of the Patrol Service. From the trawlermen the newcomers learned the art of survival at sea. They learned fast. They had to.

During the course of the 1939-45 War the Patrol Service suffered the highest number of casualties, of ships and men, of any branch of the Senior Service. It is not difficult to see why. Their's was the dangerous job of keeping the sea lanes free of mines. Throughout the fury and savagery of the war in the Atlantic the trawlers and corvettes sailed with the convoys. Each time a merchantman had the misfortune to encounter an Axis torpedo it was the trawler's job to heave-to alongside the stricken ship and attempt to recover any survivors. Stationary in the water, and silhouetted against the background of a blazing hulk, they were sitting ducks for the next torpedo.

In both the evacuation of the British Expeditionary Force from the beaches of Dunkirk, and the landing of the Allied armies on the shores of Normandy, Harry Tate's navy played a prominent part.

For many people it may have passed unnoticed that when the invasion of Europe took place the first men and ships to be exposed to the German shore batteries were those of the Patrol Service. Before the invasion fleet could approach the beaches, the mine fields, the Germans first line of defence, had to be swept clear, and the clear channels buoyed off. The trawler cum minesweepers crept in under the barrels of the German Coastal Artillery, ignored the threat of the patrolling high speed E Boats, and completed the operation. Many good trawlermen died that night, but how well they performed their task resulted in not one ship in the armada being lost through mines.

Their livelihood was destroyed at a stroke by a political decision. Officials of that same Government fed them false information that directly prejudiced their chances of receiving any compensation for their loss. Is it too much to expect the government of a prosperous nation to accept its responsibility and provide these men with a better future than a place in the dole queue?

Towns like Grimsby, Hull, Fleetwood, and the other main fishing ports owed their early growth to the advent of the steam trawler. The silver harvest of the seas that the trawlers brought home, winter and summer, was the essential ingredient that spawned, and guaranteed the continuing expansion, of the auxiliary industries: engineering, netmaking, ships chandlery, fish processing and marketing to name a few, which mushroomed around the fish docks and generated the prosperity of the local communities. Sundays and Christmas Day excepted, the trawlers discharged their catches on every day of the year, hence every day was a pay day, and the tills in the nearby shops and taverns rang out their chorus of appreciation as they digested the hard earned money the fishermen invariably handed over the counters as if there was no tomorrow, thus adding to the affluence of the local business fraternity.

However, the trawlermen were regarded by many who took their money without a qualm, as some form of lower life; a necessary nuisance to be endured for a couple of days until they had been relieved of their money, and then packed off to the hell that was the Arctic fishing grounds for another three or four weeks. A returning fisherman, on entering the bar of his usual watering hole would always, without exception, be greeted with the same two questions - "How much did you make?" and "When are you going away?"

One incident which illustrates the general, often thinly disguised, contempt in which we were held stands out.

Before it was demolished to make room for the flyover, the Royal Hotel was situated on Cleethorpes Road, Grimsby, a stone's throw from Riby Square and the main entrance to the Fish Docks. The lounge bar at the Royal, a big plushy room, was entered through a door at the right of the foyer a couple of yards from the reception desk, and was a popular rendezvous with the trawlermen. Every weekday, from noon till closing time, the place would be packed with fishermen, some alone, some with wives or girl friends. The wine would flow freely and you could always rely on finding a colleague to discuss the latest fishing reports with, a girl to wine and dine for the evening, or a companion to do the round of clubs with after the mandatory "Time, gentlemen, please" whichever way your inclinations lay.

One day, having just returned from a three-week trip to Iceland, I entered the Royal only to find that the door connecting the foyer to the lounge bar had been bricked up. Seeing me staring at the blank wall that had once been a door, the young newly appointed manager explained. "The entrance to the lounge is on the side of the building now. We've isolated it from the rest of the hotel. You know Sir, some of our guests may find the fishermen objectionable. You know what they are like."

I probably knew what they were like much better than he did and told him so. Our money was acceptable; our company wasn't. Segregation was his solution to the problem.

Just before sailing on my first trip, my Mother, who tried so hard to dissuade me from embarking on a fishing career, showed me an advert she had clipped from a local newspaper some years previously, with the comment "This is what you are giving up college for, lad." The advertisement read:

SMALL POTATOES 5d. per sack
Fit for Consumption by Pigs and Fishermen

Things hadn't changed much over the years.

A small minority of the trawlermen indulged in frequent bouts of hell raising, of one form or another, when on shore. As a consequence the majority were tarred with the same brush.

That majority formed an army of honest, hard working, hard drinking family men. Generous to a fault, they had scant regard for the value of money, and their conduct seldom conformed with that of their shore based compatriots; but then, their whole life style was far from conventional.

They spent, on average, over 340 days of each year at sea doing the toughest job on earth. Trips lasted between three and four weeks, depending on fishing and weather conditions, with a two-day turn round time between trips.

Conditions on board were intolerable at worst, primitive at best. Living quarters were cramped, all available space being allocated to fish storage space, net stores and bunker capacity; characteristics that maximized the earnings potential of the ship. There was no financial return in crew comfort so that consideration had a low priority, if it appeared on the list at all. The sides of the fish holds were insulated; the sides of the crew accommodation were not, and as a result they dripped condensation all summer and were covered with a coating of frost and ice the rest of the time. It is hardly surprising that many of the older men are now crippled with rheumatism.

From 1941 until the war finished I never sailed on a trawler that boasted a flush lavatory, running hot water, a bath or a shower. When the weather was fine the accepted method of accomplishing a bowel movement was to sit on the after bulwarks, fearnoughts round ankles, and excrete into the sea. In bad weather you used the stokehold, shovelling the excrement into the middle fire.

Facilities for washing were nonexistent. The fresh water carried was reserved for culinary purposes and for topping up the boiler. At the end of the trip there might be enough water left to warrant a bucketful each for a wash and shave before going ashore. Then the deckhands had the problem of heating it. The obvious method of putting the bucket on top of the galley stove was out. The officer's buckets occupied all the available space. One way was to put an iron shackle on the fc'sle fire before going on watch. On coming off watch you dropped the shackle, now white hot, into a bucket of cold water. Result: instant hot water. Put a mugful to one side and you had your shaving water.

After the war a number of factors combined to bring about an improvement in living conditions on the ships. In 1939 practically the entire distant water trawling fleet was requisitioned by the Admiralty and a great many of these ships had been lost through enemy action. When hostilities ceased there was a big rebuilding programme, initially financed by the compensation paid out for the lost ships, and later by a generous grant and loan scheme operated by the White Fish Authority.

Although the first of these new boats were powered by the traditional triple expansion steam engines, this method of propulsion was soon superseded by the more economical diesel engine. The new diesel powered ships needed to carry much less fuel oil so more fresh water could be loaded. The massive boiler the steam engine needed was now redundant and was replaced with a smaller boiler to provide a domestic hot water system.

Introduction of the diesel engine also allowed drastic changes to be made in interior design. The extra space created by doing away with the boiler meant that the for'ard fc'sle could be scrapped and all the men accommodated aft in two and four berth cabins. There was room for a shower and a drying room, and bunks were fitted with spring mattresses and boasted the luxury of a reading light. Now, when steaming in heavy weather, the seamen could change bridge watches without having to navigate the treacherous foredeck, clean themselves up before turning in after an 18 hour stint on deck, and enjoy the luxury of having a dry change of clothes when turning out.

One other factor played a significant part in bringing about the above improvements in living conditions aboard ship. Enemy action had depleted the number of pre-war trawlermen and those that survived returned to a country enjoying full employment. On demobilization many of them had had their fill of the sea, and had no difficulty finding work ashore. Once having sampled the comforts of life ashore, and the pleasures of spending every night under the lee of 'bum island', they were reluctant to return to the rigours of life on the trawlers. Industry had expanded around the ports that had no connection with fishing, and competed for the available labour. The I.C.I. factory at Fleetwood and the Humber Bank factories are examples. For once, the trawler owners experienced difficulty in manning their ships. The young newcomers to fishing, nicknamed commandos by the older hands, refused to accept many of the privations endured by their predecessors and trade union membership was introduced. Time in dock between trips was increased to a minimum of sixty hours, and the owners had to provide an allocation of bedding and protective clothing. A holiday pay scheme was introduced, and as a result of the Holland Martin Report, safety standards were tightened up.

But no way was ever devised of controlling the Arctic climatic conditions, and the only solution to reducing the outrageous number of hours the men were exposed to those conditions - if the ships were to work continuously for the fourteen days or so that they were on the fishing grounds - would have been to increase the size of the crews; a measure the trawler owners resisted tooth and nail.

Look at a Mercator map of the world. The fishing grounds stretch from the coasts of Newfoundland, Labrador and Baffin Island to the west, as far as the west coast of Novaya Zemlya to the east, and extend as far north as it is possible to go; that is until the Arctic ice barrier blocks any further progress. North of this line the sea is permanently frozen over, the ice so thick that even the most powerful Russian ice breakers cannot penetrate it. The perimeter of the fishing grounds encompasses the Davis Strait, the Denmark Strait and the treacherous waters round Iceland, the Greenland and Barents Seas, the Norwegian Sea and that part of the Arctic Ocean that remains unfrozen; probably the most hostile, inhospitable and violent expanses of water on the planet; for the most part uncharted, and whose only regular human visitors are the trawlermen and sealers.

During the short summer the sun never sets and, for most of the time, fog and mist prevails. Throughout the long winter months the sun never rises above the horizon in these northern latitudes and in the perpetual darkness the northern lights simmer and flash like a carpet of Roman candles, that is, on the few nights that the sky is visible through the falling snow and hail. The temperature drops below minus 40 degrees Centigrade and gale, or even hurricane, force winds howl through the rigging and turn the sea into a boiling cauldron. In these conditions, the wind-driven spray freezes on contact with the vessel, and ice builds up on the top parts that, if allowed to accumulate, seriously affects the stability of the ship, giving rise to the danger of capsizing. Then catching fish is relegated to second place. The cod will wait; the ice won't. All hands set about chopping the ice away in a desperate effort to keep their ship afloat, literally fighting for their lives. Periodically some unfortunate crew would be caught in conditions so severe that their efforts to combat the build up of ice were unavailing. The black ice would win the battle; the trawler would turn over, and twenty men would die, the blood freezing in their veins before they'd been in the water two minutes. Ashore, women would become widows and children fatherless. The local paper would carry a feature on the front page and perhaps an editorial on safety at sea. The Port Missionary would go round and distribute his cargo of sympathy and conduct a service at the Fishermen's Chapel. The trawler owner would check that his ship was adequately insured and then the job would go back to normal. Until the next time, when the procedure would be repeated. One 'next time' occurred in the late sixties when icing-up caused the loss of three ships and fifty-nine men all from Hull off northwest Iceland.

That, on the exposed foredeck, often thigh-deep in icy water, was the trawlermen's workplace.

Every fishing trip started with the passage to the fishing grounds and this part of the trip was a piece of cake compared with what was to come. Two oceans had to be traversed, the Atlantic and the Arctic, and steaming time varied between four days and a week depending on the intended destination and the weather conditions encountered.

During this time the trawl had to be fixed alongside, deck pound boards shipped in position, the fish washer assembled, the fishroom prepared to accept the expected catch, and spare fishing gear made ready, in short, all the jobs that could be done to save time when the real work on the fishing grounds started.

It was rare for the men to be required to work more than a twelve hour day, and in bad weather most of the jobs could be done in the shelter afforded by the whaleback or the fore hold; those tasks that necessitated exposure to the elements being shelved until the weather improved.

In the winter months those ships working the Barents Sea grounds would use the shelter afforded by the Norwegian fiords to ease part of the passage. Eight hundred and seventy miles northeast of the Humber they would pass Skonvar light to port and enter West Fiord. A twelve hour steam under the lee of the Lofoten Islands would bring them to the pilot station at Lodigen where they would embark a pilot for the passage through the north fiords, a twenty-four hour steam through some of the grandest scenery on earth, to Honingsvaag, where the pilot was disembarked. The voyager couldn't enjoy the scenery. The long Arctic night shrouded the view for most of the time, but the freedom from bouncing and tossing about was a luxury to be appreciated. After leaving Honingsvaag a four or five hour steam up Porsanger Fiord and they would pass between

Helsnes and Nord Kyn and enter the Barents Sea all ready for business.

On any particular trip the area to be fished, and the weather to be fished in or steamed through, were matters for the skipper to decide. He, and he alone, made the decisions, and in the eyes of the owners, and to some extent in the eyes of the crew, if he caught a good trip of fish he was a hero; if he didn't he was rubbish. In this respect there were no acceptable excuses. A couple of consecutive bad trips and the unfortunate skipper would be unceremoniously relieved of his command, and demoted to sail as mate with a more successful colleague, or to stand on the corner until the owners decided he had learned his lesson. Some of the unlucky ones spent as much, or more, time 'walking about' as they spent at sea. It was the luck of the draw, and a skipper was only as good as his last trip.

This aspect of the job, the fiercely competitive struggle to gain and retain a command, was the prime factor which instilled in the skipper the ruthlessness of purpose that demanded maximum performance from the ship, and drove men beyond the normal limits of physical endurance. It explains why, when ships engaged in a more sedate trade were running for shelter, the trawlers were steaming off to shoot their gear. It explains, even if it doesn't justify the reason why, when homeward bound, if severe weather conditions were encountered that warranted the ship being eased in or hove to in the interests of safety, the engine room telegraph stayed at Full Ahead, and ship and crew were gambled against the fury of the elements. Catching the market could make a difference of several thousand pounds to the voyage returns; the difference between success and failure; whether the ship sailed again with the same skipper or a replacement. A classic example of how market forces and safety procedures were at loggerheads.

On arrival at the fishing grounds, the real work starts. The trawl gear, which comprises the huge net, a ground rope of 24 inch diameter iron bobbins to facilitate the passage of the net over rocky ground, the heavy trawl doors that spread the net, and the necessary connecting wires and shackles, weigh several tons. It is heaved over the ship's side and lowered to the sea bed. Once on the bottom the trawl is towed along at a speed of about three knots. After a two or three hour tow it is hauled, emptied of fish, and shot away again. With a good crew, in about a hundred fathom depth of water, the entire hauling and shooting operation takes about twenty-five minutes of backbreaking labour.

After the gear is shot the first time a routine develops. The deck crew is split into four watches, three watches working on deck and one watch below. This arrangement ensures that every man works for eighteen hours a day and gets five hours sleep; the times watches are changed, being set so that meal times come from the watch below.

The trawl is hauled, emptied of fish, any damage to the gear repaired, then shot away again. During the two or three hour interval between hauling and shooting the catch is gutted, washed and packed in ice in the fish hold. Sometimes, after the fish is gutted and put to bed, there might be time to sit down and have a mug of tea and a cigarette in comfort, other times there will be too much fish to clear in the time available. This seemingly endless repetition: haul, shoot, gut the fish, haul..... will continue non-stop for the fourteen days or so that the ship is on the fishing grounds.

Only three contingencies will break this routine; a mechanical breakdown of essential machinery; a steam to another fishing ground, or weather so severe that trawling is impossible.

The main weather component that halts fishing operations is wind. Wind has to be so strong, generally above Force 9 on the Beaufort Scale, that the ship is unable to manoeuvre when working the gear; when the sea generated is so heavy that the risk of washing the entire deck crew over the side is so high as to be unacceptable, or when freezing temperatures combine with the wind to cause ice formation on the ship so that all hands are required to chop it away if the vessel is to be maintained in a stable condition. In order to reduce ice formation to a minimum the ship must be manoeuvred so that water intake is minimized, a course of action that is not possible when working the fishing gear.

Frost alone never halts the fishing. Even in temperatures of minus forty or fifty degrees Centigrade the work is able to continue. The towing block that secures the warps while towing can be cleared with a bucket of boiling water. Winch controls, frozen solid, can be freed with a steam hose and a few well directed blows with a hammer. The winch can be prevented from freezing solid by leaving it turning over the whole time between hauls, and the ropes used in the hauling operation can be dragged into the drying room until required to prevent them freezing as rigid as iron bars. That only leaves the men, and it is remarkable wnat punishment the human frame can stand, and how quickly man can adjust to a hostile environment when he has to.

The snot from running noses freezes to the top lip, icicles form on beards and eyebrows, and you keep the joints moving to combat frostbite. After mending the net, a job which is impossible to do quickly wearing mittens, I've picked up a spanner to tighten a shackle, and on putting down the spanner the flesh has come away from the palm of my hand. In these freezing conditions gutting fish is an agony. By the time the trawl is shot and gutting starts, the top layers of fish have frozen as hard as boards, too hard to get a knife into, and form a crust, leaving the inside of the pie guttable. The fish blood freezes on wrists and faces, and after gutting every three or four fish you flap your arms like a humming bird flaps its wings, and wriggle your toes and stamp your feet, to keep the circulation going. If the 'Old Man' is in a good mood he might send a bottle of rum down and that helps. Someone might say "Christ, its as cold as my old woman" and everybody will laugh, but the laugh will be humourless. There is not much to laugh at.

As the fishing continues, day after day, the effects of working an eighteen hour day, every day, begin to show. Weary from lack of adequate sleep you go through the motions oblivious of everything but the need to keep going; till one haul, about fourteen days after fishing started, when the Old Man will sing out from the bridge window "Call all hands. We're going home when we haul", and you know that the ordeal is nearly over for that trip.

Although the skipper decides where to fish, when

the trawler arrives on the fishing grounds the mate comes into his own. He is king, and the deck is his kingdom; a domain he rules with a rod of iron, which brooks interference from no man. During fishing operations his orders are obeyed without question; helm, engines and men are his to command.

Among men who admire physical attributes above all else, the mate holds the respect of the crew in a way the skipper never can. No matter how tough the going, no matter how severe the weather, he is on the storm-swept deck with them, directing operations, bellowing his commands above the howl of the gale, cajoling and driving them to greater efforts, extracting from them feats of endurance they didn't know they possessed, sparing no-one, least of all himself.

As he bounds along the slippery, heaving deck (mates never walk) with the sure footedness of a mountain goat you might hate his guts, but you respect him, and as a consequence of that respect, you bow to his authority. You respect him because, doing a highly dangerous job, he is always where the going is toughest and carries the most risk. Your hardship is his hardship, and when he curses at you and demands more from you than you think you have to give you know it is in your own interest and try to oblige. Complain to him that your hands are sore and he'll probably snarl "Do the same as I do, Sonny, piss on 'em." Cry with the cold and he'll tell you "Bring your Mummy with you next trip." Throughout the entire period on the fishing grounds he carries the ship, and as a result he carries the men with him. When the fishing has finished he'll be as nice as pie, but woe betide the man foolish enough to upset him during fishing operations.

"Call all hands. We're going home when we haul."

These words seem to raise the temperature; suddenly it doesn't feel as cold. Tired muscles draw on some hidden reserve of energy. Men laugh and joke as they gut the last few baskets of fish, stow the deck pound boards that seem about three times as heavy as when they were shipped up at the start of the trip, chop the trawl of the ground wire and heave it under the whaleback, and batten down the fishroom hatches for the last time. With all the gear stowed and secure the men troop of the deck. Deck working lights are switched of, engines rung full ahead, and the ship's head pointed south. "We're going home."

In the warmth of the accommodation block oilskins and heavy deck gear are stripped off and hung up to dry. The 'Sparks' appears with a bottle of rum, a medicine glass, and the remark "Not many ships for Tuesday, lads, so we should be all right."

The mate comes in the messroom, plonks a case of McEwans Export on the table, and sets the steaming watches. As he departs for the bridge he says pleasantly to his watchmate "Fetch some coffee up as soon as she boils, sunshine, and don't be too long", and you marvel at his transformation from snapping, snarling slave driver to pleasant, good humoured shipmate.

In the comfort of the messroom, enjoying the luxury of dry clothes, light headed from the effects of a tot of rum and a can of Export, the rigours of the last fortnight are forgotten. They had challenged the Arctic, endured all the torment nature could subject them to, and this time they'd won the battle.

All that remained was to drive the ship the 1500 miles or so to market, and in comparison with what had gone before that was easy.

The whole atmosphere on board a homeward bound trawler is markedly different to that which prevailed on the outward passage, especially so when there is a good catch stowed in the fish hold. The married men look forward to a few precious hours with wife and children; the single chaps relish the prospect of a night out with one of the girls, and if they are lucky, a session between the sheets, or on the mat in front of the fire after their darling's mother has gone to bed - a much pleasanter fate than which awaited them on the outward passage.

Bathed and shaved, they are able to relax, read a book, maybe form a solo school or have a game of cribbage in the evening, or simply enjoy an uninterrupted night's sleep with the knowledge that on waking they'd be spending the next watch within the confines of a cosy wheelhouse, perhaps listening to the latest pop music on the radio, a pot of tea or coffee close to hand, and not being called on to do an eighteen hour stint on a frozen, windswept fore deck.

There is still work to be done, plenty of it, but now the pressure is off. The trawl has to be overhauled for next trip, but that can be done under the shelter of the whaleback and there is no great urgency. Bobbin wires and the backstrops on the trawl doors have to be renewed, but they can wait for a fine day or a lee shore. Decks have to be chlorined and scrubbed to get rid of fourteen day's accumulation of fish slime, cabins and alleyways have to be spotless, mats and the Old Man's carpet has to be scrubbed, and there is all the brasswork to polish, but these chores, left till the last day at sea, are almost a pleasure because they signal the end of another trip, and herald the start of a couple of days ashore.

Every day the trawler journeys southward the days grow a little longer and the air temperature rises. She loses her coating of ice and picks up her escort of seagulls. Eventually, four or five days after leaving the Arctic she will, if Grimsby bound, round Spurn Point, navigate the Humber estuary, and drop anchor off the Lower Burcum Buoy. The section tug BRENDA FISHER will scurry alongside, exchange copies of tomorrow's landing list and today's tabloids for a tin or two of bonded Old Friend, give the skipper his berthing number, and make fast alongside to await the next arrival.

Soon the tide will rise to a level that permits the lock gates to be opened. The ships will pick up their anchors, form an orderly procession through the locks, and head towards their alloted berth on Pneumonia Quay. Heaving lines, followed by mooring ropes, will snake ashore, windlasses will chatter, moorings come taut, and as the crewmen head for the waiting fleet of taxis another trip will come to an end. An end for everyone but the mate. He has one more job to do.

At midnight the hatches will come off, and the lumpers will begin the task of discharging, sorting and weighing the fish in time for the auction which starts at 0730. Throughout the night the mate will be on the quayside 'watching his fish'. While it is the skipper's job to find the fish, the onus is on the mate to deliver it to the market in the best possible condition. Anything wrong with the quality of the fish and his job is on the line.

After the fish is sold the mate has one more task. He must go over his defects list with the foremen tradesmen, point out any faults, and advise them what he wants doing. Then the trip is over for him too.

Even when the ship lands a good trip of fish there is still no guarantee of a good pay day for the trawlermen. That depends on the price the fish makes at auction. While the deckhands and engineers receive a small wage in addition to their share of the catch, the skipper and mate are entirely dependent on the amount the fish makes for their remuneration. They have to pay for the food they eat, and repay the allotment their wives draw. If markets are bad they may have done a month's work for nothing, maybe even settling in debt. If markets are good their pay can be substantial.

About noon the men will congregate at the office, the company accountants will have totted up the ship's earnings, and the cashier will settle up with each crew member; the ratings at the window, the skipper and mate in the privacy of the inner office.

A further thirty-six hours to spend their money and sample the delights of civilization and then off to sea to do it all again; on average about fifteen times a year.

All of the following anecdotes are fact. In some cases the names of ships and people have been changed to preserve anonymity. If the book gives the reader a better understanding of what life as a trawlerman entailed, and pricks the conscience of some of those who in the past have treated them with such contempt, then I will have succeeded in my objective.

John Nicklin

Trawler heading into an Atlantic gale (Hull Docks Museum)

Chapter One

A BRIEF HISTORY

In compiling this short account of the history of trawling I am basing my story on the port of Grimsby for two reasons. Firstly, I spent most of my fishing years sailing from that port. Secondly, now living in that locality, I have access to the well documented local history archives.

The three factors that combined to transform Grimsby, a small seaside community of 1,500 souls in the year 1800, into the largest fishing port in the world, apply to the development of every main centre of the fish catching industry in the United Kingdom.

First, in 1848, came the railway, which was to enable the setting up of an efficient distribution network so essential if a highly perishable product was to be handled on a large scale.

Then, in 1857, construction of a large fish dock was completed. This dock provided the permanent base for the increasing number of fishing boats using the port. Subsidiary industries mushroomed in this new dock area, and these increased facilities, together with the discovery of new prolific fishing grounds in the Dogger Bank area, attracted an influx of vessels from the south of the country. The fishing fleet expanded to such an extent that in 1866 the fish dock had to be enlarged to twice its original size.

By 1880 over 1,000 fishing vessels were landing their catches at the port.

While the railway and dock provided the means of handling and distributing the fish, one other feature was essential for the fishing industry to expand on this scale. There had to be an adequate supply of cheap labour or 'cost-effective workforce'.

Initially the boats which brought home the fish were smacks; small fishing boats that derived their power from the wind. Life on the smacks was both hard and dangerous. In the decade 1886 to 1895, over 700 men were lost at sea from Grimsby smacks.

A large percentage of the cost-effective workforce required to crew the smacks was procured from orphanages, work houses, reformatories, Dr Barnado's homes and other institutional sources. These young lads, some only 12 years of age, were bound over to serve for five or six years, and paid about ten shillings a week. The constant flow of young boys from the institutions suited the smack owners down to the ground. It was a plentiful supply of low cost labour, and there was the added advantage that the boys had no one to keep an eye on their interests and well-being. According to a Select Committee Report in 1878, 3,480 men crewed the 600 smacks sailing from the port, and of these, 1,800 of them were bound apprentices.

There is no doubt that some skipper owners treated their charges fairly, and when not at sea, housed the lads in their own home as members of the family. It is equally certain that many boys were treated very badly indeed, being beaten, abused, and subjected to a degree of cruelty approaching inhumanity. For a few of the boys joining the smacks was the start of a successful career, and the beginning of the road to owning their own ship. For many it was the exchange of a life of hardship for one harder and more dangerous. Some of the boys were not strong enough, or were otherwise unsuitable to cope with the long trips at sea. Others found the harshness of the life, and the cruelty and abuse unbearable. They ran away.

When caught, these runaways were dragged before the magistrates' court and either returned to their vessel under escort, or sentenced to prison for up to twelve weeks. Many of them chose prison rather than a return to life on the smacks. In the five years from 1874 to 1878 over 1,000 boys from Grimsby were imprisoned in Lincoln Gaol. The following is an extract from a report in a Lincolnshire newspaper in 1873:

"The lads are brought by train, which generally arrives about 9.30 a.m. and are heavily chained together in numbers of three to five. In this way they are marched through the busiest part of the High Street of our City for more than a mile to their destination."

It is not possible to assess just how many of these lads were lost at sea because loss of life at sea did not have to be officially reported until legislation was introduced in 1880. Nor is it possible to estimate how many of the deaths were suicidal rather than accidental, the boys preferring death to a continuation of life on the smacks.

As the number of boats increased, fish stocks in the waters around the Humber and Lincolnshire coast began to decline and the fishermen were forced to go further afield. Boats began to venture to the northern parts of the North Sea, to the Faroes, Iceland and Greenland, most of them fishing with lines, this method of fishing being less dependent on the wind than trawling. The Board of Trade rightly considered that to voyage to these more distant waters a higher standard of navigation was required and in 1880 introduced an oral examination for skippers and mates' certificates. Those men already serving were granted Certificates of Servitude.

At the same time the Merchant Shipping Act of 1880 ruled that men and boys should not be sent to prison for deserting a fishing boat. The purpose of this ruling was to prevent the owners of fishing vessels from using the courts to man their ships, but in this respect it was only partially successful. The owners found ways of getting round the Act and fishermen were still taken to court. In the two years between the introduction of the Act and 1882 280 boys from Grimsby served prison sentences in Hull Gaol.

But the number of boys signing indentures was beginning to decline each year, and by 1882 the number of apprentices had dropped to 800, with over 1,000 weekly paid hands being employed to make up the shortfall.

At that time, 25 per cent of the boys being indentured were breaking their agreement, and a greater number of weekly paid hands had to be signed on. This was not to the owner's liking. They preferred the apprentice system. The boys were cheaper to come by, were easier to control, and could be owned body and soul. The ship owners from Grimsby, Hull, and Great Yarmouth sent a deputation to meet the President of the Board of Trade in an attempt to enlist his support and to convince him that the apprentice system was vital to the continued growth of the fishing industry.

They failed. Mr. Joe Chamberlain, President of the Board of Trade at that time, offered them little sympathy, and expressed the official view that sending young boys to prison was not an acceptable way of retaining the work force. He criticized the cruelty doled out to the lads, comparing their conditions to those that existed in the slave trade, and suggested that an improvement in working conditions, and the application of a little more humanity in the treatment of the youngsters, was a more desirable way to keep them in the industry.

Following the deputation the owners wrote to the Board of Trade complaining that to abolish the apprentice system would be catastrophic for the industry, but the complaint fell on deaf ears, and the number of apprentices continued to decline. The shortfall had to be made up by the use of weekly paid hands, labour considered by the owners to be inferior to the apprentices.

While many of the skipper owners of the smacks were of intemperate habits, and squandered their hard earned money on hard liquor, and the softer distractions offered by those houses of ill-fame that spring up in any boom town, there were others of a more prudent disposition. They saved their money, and over a long period of time became very wealthy men. They built big houses, owned their own horses and carriages, employed domestic servants, and investing in the fishing, became the owners of considerable numbers of fishing smacks. These men laid the foundations of the future trawling empires.

The practice of 'fleeting' was introduced, those owners with a number of ships under their management sending their boats to sea in a group under the command of a Fleet Admiral. Carrier boats made regular trips to the fishing grounds to collect the catch, and delivered the fresh fish direct to Billingsgate Market. This fleet fishing meant that the crews had to remain at sea for up to three months or more, had less shore leave, and had to work harder. It made an already highly dangerous job even more hazardous, especially so when the fish had to be transferred to the carrier in foul weather by rowing boat. The captain of the carrier was always in a hurry to load and depart to catch the market, and the injury and death rate of the fishermen was high.

Apart from the hazards created by the nature of the work, another factor played a part in the increasing casualty rate. The 'Coper' ships, sailing from the Dutch ports, made regular visits to the fishing fleets to exchange clothing, tobacco and booze for fish. As the size of the fishing fleets increased the number of copers increased also, and there was always one of them in the vicinity of the fleet. Being free of duty, the tobacco and liquor they had to barter was cheap, and drunkenness among the fishing boat crews reached epidemic proportions. Alcoholism must have been a contributory factor in many of the cases of death or injury.

Mr. E.J. Mather was a man of high moral standing, and a genuine humanitarian. After making several trips with the fleeters he wrote the book 'Nor'ard Of The Dogger'. Distressed by the conditions they worked under, the perils they faced daily, and their apparent lack of Christian morals, he determined to start a crusade in aid of the physical and spiritual well being of those unfortunates. Largely due to his efforts, and public donations, a 56 ton yawl, the Ensign, was provided by Hewitt and Company. Equipped with warm clothing, a supply of medical and first aid equipment, and a load of literature supplied by the Bible Society, the Church of England and other religious bodies, the Ensign sailed from Yarmouth and headed for the fishing grounds. The Mission to Deep Sea Fishermen was born. At first the Ensign was greeted with a mixture of ridicule and scorn by the men she was seeking to help, the fishermen preferring the visits of the floating grog shops, but gradually, after treating many casualties, tending to sometimes horrible injuries, and conducting religious services at sea, the hand of friendship the Ensign offered was grudgingly accepted. By the middle of the eighteen eighties the Mission had four more of these mercy ships operating. They carried a supply of cheap duty free tobacco and later W.D. & H.O. Wills took over the job of supplying the smokes at production cost only. These vessels of goodwill became welcome visitors to Dogger Bank, and the merchandise they carried did much to reduce the trade of the copers. Drunkenness reduced with the reduction of the supply of booze, less fishing time was lost, and the rate of alcohol induced accidents declined.

But the days of iron men and wooden ships were coming to a close.

In the early eighteen seventies a Mr. Fred Rushworth ordered an iron hulled vessel from a Hull shipbuilder, initially to be operated under sail but designed for later conversion to steam. This boat, the Tubal Cain, was registered at Grimsby in May 1874 and was 77.7 feet long and 111 tons gross. As a fishing smack she made several good voyages to northern waters under sail, but within three or four years her sails were replaced with a steam engine and a propeller. This experiment was not a success and a little later she was lengthened and a new steam engine was fitted. These modifications worked and the vessel made highly profitable voyages to the Faroes, landing huge catches, and cutting down the time on outward and homeward passages drastically. The Tubal Cain, watched with interest by the owners of the smack fleet, demonstrated that the iron built steam trawler was better able to withstand the storms, and in periods of calm was able to effectively pull the trawl while her sisters under sail were idle. The age of the steam trawler had arrived. Tubal Cain continued to fish from Grimsby until August 1898 when she sank off Flamborough Head after a collision with the Newcastle steamer Admiral Nelson.

In 1881, the Great Grimsby Steam Fishing Company was formed with a capital of £50,000 and the Company's first four ships, called after signs of the zodiac - the Aries, Leo, Taurus, and Zodiac were trawling by 1883.

The change over from sail to steam was rapid. By 1890 forty-two steam trawlers were fishing from the port. Two years later the number was one hundred and thirteen. In order to catch a similar quantity of fish the trawlers needed fewer men than the smacks, and the increase in the number of steamships, and the corresponding decrease in the size of the sailing fleet, resulted in a growing pool of men seeking work. Ideal conditions for nurturing a low pay labour force. With pay little above starvation level, and with the employers' enthusiasm to invoke the courts to enforce their harsh conditions, often with a shipowner the presiding magistrate, labour relations in the industry were never good.

Fishermen were becoming increasingly rebellious and attempts at forming a trade union were made. Early in 1892 the cod line fishermen went on strike for better pay. The strike was doomed to failure and very short lived. The owners converted the liners to trawl fishing and imported crews from other ports. After three weeks the strike collapsed, but when the strikers decided to go back to sea they found there were no jobs for them. With an increasing pool of surplus labour the owners were able to blacklist them, and at the same time dictate terms to those men lucky enough to have a berth on one of the boats.

By 1900, steam trawlers were being delivered from the shipyards at a rate of 100 ships a year and although the rate slowed down considerably, new boats continued to arrive at the port every year until the outbreak of the Great War in 1914. With the ascendancy of steam over sail the era of the one boat skipper-owner passed into decline. The new steam trawlers cost about £4,000 to build, a tidy sum in those days, and to raise the necessary capital companies were being formed.

In 1901, the expanding industry suffered a hiccup. The apprentice system had gone, and with the disappearance of that source of cheap labour, the rapidly increasing fleet of trawlers had to be manned almost entirely with weekly paid hands. Trawlers were expensive to build and operate and many of the owners of single, or two or three boats, were feeling a financial pinch. After a series of meetings they decided that the root cause of their difficulties was that they were paying the fishermen too much. Fishermen's earnings had to be reduced. They banded together to form the Grimsby Federated Owners' Protection Society Limited, set up new rates of pay for fishermen, and refused to sign men on the trawlers except at the new terms offered.

Under the new terms the weekly wage was drastically reduced, and was supplemented with a small share of the value of the catch. Their reasoning was that by paying a part of the men's wages as a share of the catch it would encourage them to work harder, and at the same time, by manipulating the accounts, they could reduce the poundage paid out to an insignificant level.

The fishermen, who already considered that they were overworked and underpaid, refused to accept the wage cut en masse and from the beginning of July the trawlers were laid up as they arrived in port. Soon over 400 trawlers were laid up in Grimsby Dock.

The dispute was peaceful at first, but when the owners attempted to import foreign seamen to man the ships, bitter, starving men went on the rampage. Rioting broke out on the Fish Docks and the Federation offices were wrecked. Police from Sheffield and Manchester, and soldiers from the Lincolnshire Regiment were drafted into the town, and the Riot Act was read out in Riby Square. Shortly after this, in October, the men were starved back to sea on the owners' terms. Those terms, with little change, remained in force until after World War II (1947).

By the end of the first decade of the twentieth century the transition from sail to steam was complete. The 1,000 smacks that had worked from Grimsby in the heyday of sail had been replaced by over 500 steam trawlers which brought home twice the amount of fish. According to Edward Drury in The Great Grimsby Story (self published circa 1990) by 1909 there were 680 ships fishing from the port, and of these, 654 were steam driven.

With the increased catching power many of the fishing grounds being trawled began to show signs of overfishing, and to maintain the big catches the boats had to venture further and further afield. New fishing grounds were discovered in the White Sea (Barents Sea), and some boats were voyaging as far as the coasts of Newfoundland and Labrador in the search for cod, and to Morocco for soles. With longer voyages, and bigger catches, bigger ships were needed, and the average length of the new trawlers coming from the yards was over 120 feet.

In order to service this massive fleet of trawlers the allied trades boomed. Dry docks and coaling facilities were needed; ship repairers, engineering shops and metal working trades expanded; an ice factory replaced the previous method of importing ice from the frozen lakes of Norway; sail and net makers, box and basket makers, and ships chandlers all enjoyed the boom; and the ships had to be provisioned, and the fishermen clothed at sea and ashore. The fish they landed had to be processed and distributed. The entire prosperity of the community became dependent on what came up in the fisherman's net, and the regularity with which his catch was brought home. That fish was the lifeblood of the town. Without it the town would sink into mediocrity.

The trawlers of that day had no radio communications, and once they left the Humber no one knew where they were until they returned. Success or failure, then as always, depended on the skill of the skipper, and the expertise of the men working on deck. There was still a heavy price to pay for the fish, both in ships and men, because although the ships were bigger and better able to stand up to the weather, they were venturing into the unknown, and the owners expected vessels and crews to be pushed to the limits of endurance and beyond. And if a skipper was disinclined to demonstrate this ruthlessness there were plenty of men ashore willing to replace him. Safety and market forces made incompatible bed mates.

In 1911, the Royal Naval Trawler Section (R.N.R.) was formed and at the outbreak of the war one hundred trawlers were requisitioned by the Admiralty in the first two weeks, Lowestoft being the minesweeping and fitting out base. By the summer of 1916 so many trawlers had been lost, and so few were left to requisition, that the Admiralty began a trawler building programme. These ships were to be initially used for minesweeping, and then sold off for fishing after the war.

In 1917, a report on the state of the trawler fleet was published which stated that without immediate action being taken, due to the high rate of losses, it would cease to exist. Of a total United Kingdom fleet of nineteen hundred trawlers at the start of the war, fifteen hundred had been drafted into Admiralty service. In the course of the war the cost to Grimsby alone was two hundred and sixteen ships and nearly eleven hundred men.

After the war the Admiralty built ships were sold off to fishing interests, and these boats formed the nucleus of the near and middle water trawling fleet. Trawler building was resumed on a considerable scale, the peak years being 1928, 1930, 1933, and 1936. Many of the later buildings were taken over by the navy as soon as they were built.

The inter war years saw radical changes on the fish docks. The cost of operating bigger trawlers, sailing to more distant grounds, was increasing. Fishing was big business requiring a large amount of capital. The smaller companies began to amalgamate, forming larger units. After taking control of their smaller brethren, the now large companies stopped fighting and trying to bankrupt each other, and under the umbrella of the various port Fishing Vessel Owners Associations (F.V.O.A.) they set up a fund to begin the process of buying out the service industries. Complete control of the fish docks, to be exploited to their mutual advantage, being the ultimate goal.

After the World War II this process continued. A small number of large companies owned or managed big fleets. Fish auctioning, trawler insurance, engineering and ship repairing, bunkering, fish meal and cod liver oil production, net making, chandlery and provisioning, and all the other services that are necessary to keep a fleet of ships at sea were gradually taken over by the trawler owning cartel. Control of the industry was eventually established to the extent that practically every penny of the wealth that dropped out of the fishermen's nets was locked within the perimeter of the fish docks, and by one route or another found its way into the trawler owners' coffers. They controlled the industry, and they controlled the lives of the people that worked in it.

From 1949, when the size of the trawler crews were cut down, the number of men seeking work on the distant water trawlers was greater than the number of berths available. For skippers, mates, or deckies, the power of the 'sack' was the weapon used to keep them toeing the line. Speak out of turn and you got the sack. Complain you were tired and you got the sack. Call the skipper a stormy bastard (and let him hear you) and you were looking for a job when the ship docked. Get on the wrong side of the ship's husband and you 'walked about'. When age caught up with you, and you weren't quite as agile, you got the sack and were grateful for a couple of trips a year at those times of the year when the regulars wanted to be ashore. Finally you ended up doing the odd day's work around the dock if you knew the right people. Or just disappeared altogether. Many a good ex-trawler hand finished their working days cleaning out the lavatories in the local fish processing factories. Maybe these were the lucky ones. Many of the men, crippled with rheumatism, didn't work at all, and on sailing morning you'd see them on 'tobacco row' begging an ounce of shag, or down the fo'c'sle of a ship due to sail on the tide, knowing there would be a dram and a can offered them by an ex-colleague, and grateful for the generous hospitality offered freely. Clear of the romanticism induced by nostalgia, that was the reality of distant water trawling in the post war years.

At the end of World War II the pay system was unchanged from that imposed by the Federation after the 1901 lock out, and the rates were very little better. A deckhand received £4.9s per week wages, but half of this amount was due to a 'war risk' payment. He also received poundage of twopence ha'penny on every pound of the ship's net earnings (1.04%). With the abolition of the war risk component a new pay structure was introduced. The weekly wage was increased to £7.10s, and the poundage was altered to £6 per £1,000 of gross earnings (0.6%). The remuneration of skippers and mates remained unchanged at 10 per cent and 7$\frac{1}{8}$ per cent of net earnings respectively.

Later the pay scales for Grimsby skippers and mates was changed. The Grimsby fleet was composed of a greater number of vessels working the near water grounds than those sailing to distant waters. Practically all these near water boats were coal burners, and the high post war cost of coal meant that after an initial boom, when the North Sea teemed with fish, expenses were so high that they were barely being cleared. From the point of view of the skippers and mates it was hardly worth taking the ships to sea. The Owners' Association offered new terms; 5 per cent for skippers and 3$\frac{1}{2}$ per cent for mates based on gross earnings. A vote on the new terms offered was taken at the Trawler Officers' Guild, and because the majority of members were North Sea men it was decided to accept the new proposed rates. Although the new deal was to the advantage of the near water men, it amounted to a pay cut for the distant water men whose grossings were substantially higher. In Hull, where the fleet was composed entirely of distant water ships, method of payment was unchanged.

In the post war trawler building boom, made necessary by the heavy losses inflicted by enemy action, the first ships delivered from the yards were powered by the traditional triple expansion steam engines, although oil replaced coal as fuel. Later steam propulsion was ousted by the more economical diesel engine.

Apart from the tremendous technological advances made in electronic navigation and fish finding equipment, the only other changes to the distant water fishing industry was the gradual introduction of a few large stern trawlers which were designed to freeze their catch at sea. These ships, well over 200 feet in length and close to 2,000 tons gross, enabled the men to gut the fish under cover out of the worst of the Arctic weather. This advantage was counter balanced by the fact that they remained at sea for much longer periods, sometimes up to three months.

Then came the Icelandic Cod Wars, and the subsequent laying up and decommissioning of the entire fleet. An entire industry, and a way of life, died almost over night.

The North Wall, once the scene of frantic activity,

and the mooring place of over a hundred ships, fitting out, storing, or waiting to sail, is now an almost deserted strip of concrete flanking an equally deserted dock. The trawlers have all gone, most of them to the breakers yard. What fishing is left in Grimsby is done by small fishing boats the size of the smacks which used the port in the days of sail in the nineteenth century. Most of them are built of wood and are skipper owned. Only the method of propulsion has changed. The wheel has turned full circle.

An early photo of Elf King (c.1913). After the Great War, she moved from Hull to Grimsby (Nov., 1918) and was re-registered as GY 1247.

Sou'wester weather. Clearing fish off the deck in a storm (Hull Docks Museum).

Chapter Two

LIFE ON THE TRAWLERS

I started my fishing career during the war at the age of fifteen and spent the greater part of the next forty five years afloat. During that time I sailed on just about every class of steam trawler; ships ranging from one hundred and twenty foot home water sidewinders with a gross tonnage of about two hundred tons to factory freezer stern trawlers with a tonnage nearer to two thousand. Over those years I have fished on every fishing ground the British trawler worked, and served in every deck capacity from 'brassie' to skipper. I have no regrets.

It is hardly surprising I went to sea. My father was a trawler skipper, and all the male members of my family were either fishermen, or working in some occupation closely connected with the trawlers. Brought up in an environment that reeked with the odour of fish and tarry twine, and living not much further than a stone's throw from the fish docks, I hankered after a job on the trawlers from an early age, an ambition my mother tried very hard to discourage.

In pre-war Fleetwood there wasn't much work to be had outside the fishing industry, and many young lads started work as 'brassies' (as the apprentice fishermen were called) when they left school at fourteen. My father was sailing as mate at the time,

and from the age of ten my summer holiday took the form of a pleasure trip, often accompanied by a school friend, on whichever trawler he was serving on. I believe my mother allowed me to go on those trips because she thought that if I had first hand experience of what the job entailed, it would banish any inclinations I might harbour towards a life at sea. It didn't work out like that.

At the age of fifteen I packed up my studies at the Harris Institute of Technology, where I was studying for an O.N.C. in engineering, to find work on the trawlers.

My father had enlisted in the Navy at the start of the war, and I had two younger brothers still at school. His Majesty's Government was not over generous in setting the rates of pay for members of the armed forces, so money was not over plentiful at home, otherwise I might have had to overcome stouter maternal opposition to my decision to leave college.

Before joining the Service my father had been working for H. Markham Cook, a Grimsby company that had moved to Fleetwood at the start of the war, and I had met the General Manager, Mr. Fred Rickardson, on several occasions. He could not have been more helpful. After first confirming that I had parental approval, he took me down to the Pool Office and introduced me to Jim Moon, Markham

Cook's ships husband, and I was signed on as brassie on the trawler Strathblair there and then. After I had signed my name on the log book, Mr. Moon commented, "If you turn out as good as your old man you'll do, John." I was to hear that remark repeated often during the learning years.

After I had signed on, Mr. Rickardson took me to the F.F.V.O.A.` stores, and saw to it that I was fitted out with a full set of sea gear, including a mattress and blanket. The outfit comprised an oilskin frock, thigh boots, sou'wester, fearnoughts, seaboot stockings, two jerseys, duffle coat, cap, mufflers and a gutting knife. That lot must have cost a pretty penny, but I was never charged for it. I can only assume that Fred passed the bill through Markham Cook's accounts although the Strathblair was not one of that company's ships. Years later I sailed for that company, then renamed Northern Trawlers, for over twenty years, thus passing on a return on that investment.

At the start of the war all the better ships were requisitioned by the Admiralty, and those boats that remained fishing were on their last legs. Strathblair came in that category. Built by Hall Russel at Aberdeen in 1905, flush decked, 110 feet long, with a gross tonnage of 193 tons, she was operated by Bloomfields Ltd., and little different to the several other trawlers I helped crew during the war years. The only reason I remember her is that she was the first trawler I sailed on as a paid hand. My starting pay was one pound five shillings a week, plus an extra twenty-one shillings a week war risk money. Some trips later, following a satisfactory report from the skipper, I also received poundage at a rate of one penny for every pound of the ship's net earnings.

At four o' clock on the morning after I had signed on I was hunking my gear aboard the Strathblair. One hour later we passed through the Wyre Dock locks, cleared Tigers Tail, and steamed up the river. We rounded Wyre Light just as dawn was breaking, and headed into the Irish Sea. The long process of my becoming an efficient trawler hand had started.

Strathblair had a crew of twelve: skipper, mate, bosun, four deckhands, chief and 2nd engineers, a fireman and a cook. As on most ships at that time you could divide the men into two age groups - those too young for service in the navy, and those too old. Although trawling was a reserved occupation, almost all the eligible men had enlisted. In fact, many of them had falsified their age, up or down, to be able to join the party, and the Admiralty needed experienced seamen too badly to make stringent checks in this respect.

Living quarters were extremely cramped. I lived with the four deckhands in the for'ard fo'c'sle. This was a triangular shaped room, about twelve feet long, and at its widest, ten feet wide, sited on top of the fore peak tank and anchor chain locker. There was just sufficient headroom to stand upright. The steel plating either side of the bow formed two of the sides, and the bulkhead at the after end formed the third side, and separated the living space from the net stores.

Like space, furniture was minimal. Six bunks, double banked, four on the port side and two on the starboard side, took up most of the room. A battery of six small lockers, two wooden bench type seats running along half the length of the bunks that served as steps to climb into the upper bunk, an iron coal stove, and a coal box completed the picture. Spare seaboots were stowed under the bunks, and the spare bunk served as a depository for our sea bags. Half a dozen nails knocked into the after bulkhead served as pegs for hanging oilskins, and a couple of lengths of twine strung up athwartships at the after end, and not too far from the stove, provided clothes lines for drying wet gear. Our one luxury was a triangular piece of tatty coconut matting that covered the wooden deck.

Although five of us lived in that small space, there was rarely more than three of us at home at any time, two of the deckhands always being on watch, and between 6 a.m. and 6 p.m. the only times I came for'ard was when I had to mend the fire. This was just as well because there wasn't room to swing a mouse, let alone a cat.

All hands took their meals in the saloon aft in two sittings. A large table, fitted with battens and with its legs bolted to the deck, took up all the after end of the saloon. Along the fore and aft sides of the table were leather covered benches backed by storage lockers. Above the lockers were four bunks, two each side, for the 2nd engineer, bosun, cook and fireman.

The mate and chief engineer each had a small cabin situated at the fore end of the saloon. A coal stove and two brass oil lamps hung in gimbals provided our final concession to civilized living. The skipper enjoyed the privacy of a small cabin under the wheelhouse.

Although I have described the living quarters aboard the Strathblair, that description could well apply to 95 per cent of the trawlers fishing from wartime Britain.

The work was hard and the hours were long. All the time I was in Strathblair we fished in the Minch, the time to get there taking, on average, about twenty-four hours. As soon as the ship cleared the locks the men were divided into two watches, two deckhands being on watch with the mate, the other two with the bosun. I was on day work from 6 a.m. to 6 p.m..

While on passage, the day was split into five watches: 0630 to 1230, 1230 to 1830, 1830 to 2300, 2300 to 0300, and 0300 to 0630. This meant that the watchkeepers had different watches on consecutive days, and one day worked fourteen hours, and ten the next. Meals were set to coincide with the times watches were changed. You took your meal either before going on watch, or when coming off. This meant that the time taken to eat your meal came off your watch below, and not off the ship's time.

The deck work started at first light as soon as the ship left the dock, one of the deckhands acting as helmsman, the other working on deck with the brassie. Always the first job was to stow the meat away. When delivered, the joints of meat would have been thrown down to the deck from the quayside, and as often as not would be covered with coal dust. First the joints had to be washed with the deck hose. There were no refrigerators aboard the ships in those days so the meat was dropped down the fish hold and buried in the ice used to stow the catch. In some home water boats, where trips could be expected to last no longer than fifteen days, and in all the foreign going ships where trips could last for anything from twenty-one to twenty-eight days, the cook would sort out several pieces of beef and pork. He would preserve these joints in brine to be used towards the end of the trip. I never liked the salt jerky, as it was called, but I suppose it was better than the rancid stuff it would have become after three weeks had it not been salted.

After checking and stowing away the various items of fishing gear and deck stores that had come aboard, the next job was to get the fish hold ready to accept the expected catch. The fishroom is the biggest compartment aboard a trawler. A central alley or stage about four or five feet wide runs down the middle, the space on either side being divided into pounds which are not unlike the stalls in a stable, except that the fronts and sides are formed with removable boards which slot into grooves in the stanchions that extend vertically from the floor to the underside of the deck.

While in dock, after the catch has been unloaded, the for'ard pounds in the fishroom are filled with crushed ice, eighty tons or more, and this ice fuses into a solid mass. Preparing the fishroom is hard work, and takes most of the day. First the sides are washed down with diluted disinfectant, all the fish slime being removed with energetic application of a stiff hand brush. Then the whole is given a good wash down with a high pressure hose, the slush well is cleaned out, a clean rose box fitted, and all the drain channels cleared. Then the duty engineer pumps the hold dry and checks the pump lines. Next, bottom boards are fitted in the six or eight after pounds, these boards resting on battens placed about three inches above the concrete floor to allow drainage. Finally, sufficient ice has to be cracked and shovelled aft, enough to put a bottom about the blade of a shovel deep in each of the prepared pounds.

After the fishroom has been made ready, the bridles - wires that connect the trawl doors to the net - are heaved on to the winch and shackled up to the gear, and all the other bits and pieces used during fishing operations are brought out and placed ready. The last job, if there is time, is to ship the deck pound boards, but this task can always be done after the trawl has been shot if necessary.

On arrival at the fishing ground the trawl is heaved over the side of the boat and lowered to the seabed and the real work starts. Depending on the amount of fish being caught, and the nature of the ground over which the trawl is being towed over, towing time will be between two and four hours duration. When there is plenty of fish about, or when the seabed is rough or 'catchy' the tows tend to be short; on fine ground with fish scarce, tows are longer, and these factors decide how much sleep, if any, the men get.

The average time the trawler will be on the fishing ground is about twelve days. During this time, although the men remain in the same watches as when on passage, the time the gear is hauled determines when the off duty watch turns in.

All the deck crew are needed to haul and shoot the gear. After the catch has been heaved aboard and the net shot away again, the fish has to be gutted, washed and sorted, and stowed away in ice down the fishroom. Only when the fish is stowed away can the watch below turn in. With long tows and slack fishing they might get three hours sleep; with short tows or plenty of fish, it might be hauling time before the work is done. If the watch below is off the deck for one hour or more that constitutes a watch below, and next haul it is the other watch's turn to have a nap. It goes without saying, that under these working arrangements, an unbroken spell of thirty-six or forty hours work on deck was not uncommon. When we did get the chance of a nap we stripped off oilskins and seaboots, but never our fearnoughts. For the entire time the ship was fishing the only times our trousers came off was when they were wet through and had to be changed. The reason for this is fairly obvious. We never knew what time we would be called out. Although, by checking the time the gear was shot, we would have a good idea what time it would be hauled, it could come fast on an obstruction at any time. If no such mishap occurred the watch would be called five minutes before hauling time, and would have to be at their working stations by the time the trawl doors came up. On being called, if we were quick we had time to get to the galley and grab a mouthful of tea before we were needed; we certainly wouldn't have the time to dress up for a party. True, when working on fine ground, we could ask the watch to call us earlier, thus giving us more time to get rigged, but during fishing operations sleep was a scarce and precious commodity, and we tried to steal every minute we could. We never knew when we would be turning in again.

One method of stealing a gash hour of Bo Peep (sleep) was as follows: during the daylight hours the mate would always find a job to keep the watch occupied, but throughout the night watches the duties merely consisted of tending the fires in the fo'c'sle, saloon and galley, keeping an eye on the marks on the trawl warps and periodically tightening the winch brakes as they cooled down, and brewing the tea and calling the watch below at hauling time. During these night watches the two deckies on watch would work what they called a tipple. One of them would attend to all the duties, while the other found a quiet corner and snatched forty winks. When it was your turn to tipple you couldn't take your gear off because if the trawl came fast you had to be immediately available, one man at the towing block to release the trawl warps, the other to ship the winch clutches and commence heaving. Nevertheless, it was bliss to be able to squat down and close our eyes.

There was no formal training on the job. By working with the men, and doing the menial tasks that required little or no skill, the newcomer gradually developed his sealegs. He was shown the safe places to stand when the trawl warps were being hove in or payed away, or when heavy bags of fish were being heaved aboard, and shown what he had to do to assist the hauling and shooting operation. From then on he learned by watching the experts, and playing on the good-natured generosity of the deckhands, who would be willing to give tuition when they were on watch and had nothing else to do, always provided he was keen, and kept them supplied with a mug of tea.

And to cross the divide between decky learner and decky there was a hell of a lot to learn. With large crews you can afford to carry a passenger or two providing you have three or four hands that can do those jobs that require a degree of skill, but aboard a trawler we had the bare number of men required to do the job. An incompetent hand placed an intolerable burden on the rest of the crew. Besides being a risk to himself and others when working the gear in heavy weather, he would have few friends aboard the ship, and could be assured of the sack when the trip finished. Whether a man was a saint or an assassin was of little consequence; his esteem in the eyes of his shipmates depended entirely on his competence on the deck.

After the demise of the distant water trawlers, I spent twelve years as first mate on merchant ships, and comparing the two jobs, the trawlermen are the finest seamen afloat in every aspect of a seaman's work, with the exception of painting, a job which occupies most of a merchant seaman's time, and which a trawlerman has neither time nor inclination to do.

As brassie, I was everybody's runaround. I had to sweep up the fo'c'sle every day, tend the coal stove throughout the daytime, and keep the coal box full. The needle basket was also my responsibility. Synthetic fibres for making fishing nets were still in the future, and the trawls were constructed of sisal and manilla twine. The trawl is a complicated piece of equipment built up with sections of net with varying mesh sizes. The local lassies, generally working for piecework rates, either at home or at the networks, braid these sections. These sections are then put together by highly skilled net fixers, more often than not ex-trawlermen, to form the complete trawl. Before being delivered to the ship the net had to be dipped in a bath of bituminous preservative to prevent rotting, as was the twine used for net mending.

The needle basket contained about four dozen braiding needles, and it was my job to see that they were kept loaded with twine, some filled with single twine for mending the net, some with double twine for lacing jobs. When each needle was filled it was rubbed down with tallow. This lubrication served a triple purpose; in use, the greased needle slipped through the messes more easily, the twine came off the needle more smoothly and was easier on the fingers, and the tar on the twine which stained your hands black was easier to scrub off. When the net was damaged I handed out the full needles, and collected and refilled the empties.

The quicker the fish could be gutted and stowed away, the more time the watch below had for sleep, so it was essential that we learned to gut fish at an acceptable speed. There is an art to picking up a live fish and removing its engine, and the experienced men could keep up a steady rate of ten to twelve fish a minute for hour after hour. For a start, I was given the coley tusk, ling and other less valuable species to operate on, but it was several trips before I acquired the knack and could earn my keep in this department.

Every haul, when the fish were nearly gutted, I had to go down the morgue, as the fish hold was called, and chop ice for the mate to use in the stowing process. This job was hard physical work, especially so when you were working the ice from the back of a pound, and there was a big haul of fish. The ice, which seemed hard as concrete, had to be chopped down, and then shovelled on to the stage. Then it had to be moved aft to where the mate would be working. The exertion made you sweat, but at least we were out of the weather.

One incident occurred in those early days still makes makes me chuckle, although the mate didn't appear to think it funny. On this particular trip we had been catching big hauls of cod that were full of roe. Roes were usually stowed away in muslin bags, bags of gold we called them, but we had run out of muslin so were stowing them in bulk in one of the underfoots below the centre stage. The previous haul, the mate had just taken the baskets of roes and tipped them into the underfoot, just filling it, when the gear came fast, and we had to hurry out of the fishroom. The next haul, when the fish was nearly gutted, I went down the fishroom and used what ice was on the stage to ice off the full underfoot of roes. Then, neglecting to replace the boards on the full underfoot, I went into the ice pound and set about chopping ice. About ten minutes later, I was merrily shovelling ice on to the stage when I heard a horrible scream. Climbing out of the ice pound to investigate the cause of the uproar I found that Harry Tate had stood on the roes and sank to the bottom. Only his head, cap still perched at a jaunty angle, protruded above the surface of the slimy, now mainly squashed, mass of roes. The mate was a big man, and despite all my efforts I couldn't extract him from the quagmire of fish eggs. Answering my call for assistance, the bosun dropped down the fishroom, but even with both of us pulling together on his arms, we couldn't get him out. It was like he was stuck in a pot of glue. As a last resort the gilson wire was lowered down the hatch, and we used the winch to heave him out. Hanging on to the wire, he came out of the underfoot with a sucking noise like water gurgling down a sink, completely covered in roe juice from chin to toenails, and minus one boot stocking and both thigh boots. With the bosun trying to keep a straight face, what the mate said to me is unprintable. I kept out of his way as much as possible for the next couple of days, but the rest of the lads kept the pot boiling. For the next couple of trips, every time I made to go down the fishroom one of them would call out, with a grin "Don't forget to put the lids on the underfoots, Johnny."

In the home water boats you were never more than about thirty-six hours steaming time from port, so the work of cleaning the ship up for docking started a day or two before fishing finished, this work generally having to be done in the night watches, thus putting an end to the afore mentioned tipple. The men took a pride in bringing the ship into dock in as clean a condition as possible. One of my jobs was to clean and polish all the brasswork until it gleamed. One ship I served in had a brass plate fixed to the after bulkhead in the wheelhouse, not unlike those plates you see screwed to the wall outside doctors' and dentists' surgeries. This plate had once sported the name of the builder and the place and date the ship was built, but time and the frequent application of Brasso and elbow grease had long since erased this information. Its only function at that time was to provide a shaving mirror for the Old Man.

It was my first trip in the ship, towards the end

of the last afternoon watch before we docked, and I was industriously polishing the brass plate. We had a good trip down the fishroom and the mate, who was on watch, was in a good mood.

"Why don't you paint that thing, Johnny" he said jokingly, "Save you a lot of work in the long run."

I considered this advice, and concluded that the suggestion was a pearl of wisdom. After tea I returned to the wheelhouse armed with a one inch paint brush and a drop of green paint I'd been able to scrounge off the chief engineer. Ten minutes later the glittering brass plate was transformed into a rectangle of emerald velvet. I missed the grins exchanged between the bosun and his watchmates, but I should have been wary at the readiness with which the chief parted with his brush and paint. As a rule, trying to beg gear off the black squad was the equivalent of getting blood out of a stone. When they did part with anything they usually wanted an arm or a leg in exchange.

The storm broke next morning when the skipper came up to the bridge to shave. I wasn't there, thank God, but I heard an account from the helmsman later that morning.

"I'd keep away from the bridge till he cools down, Snacker" he said. "He'd lathered his face before he noticed his mirror had changed colour. He nearly turned the air blue, and steam came out of his ears."

Just prior to docking I was packing my heavy gear in the fo'c'sle.

"Not packing up, are you?" one of the deckies asked.

"Not from choice" I answered "but it's a cert I'll get the sack."

"Don't worry, Kid," he said "he won't sack you."

"At least, not until you've scraped all the paint off his mirror." someone chipped in.

They were right on both counts. I didn't get the sack, and the next trip all my spare time had to be spent working on that brass plate until it had been restored to its former glory. In a lifetime working aboard trawlers that was the only occasion I wielded a paint brush. Merchant seamen please note.

Fleetwood is a tidal port, and in order to keep enough water in Wyre Dock to allow the ships to stay afloat at any state of the tide big watertight gates are fitted to the locks at the entrance. As the tide ebbs and flows, these gates are opened and closed at the discretion of the dockmaster. There are two tides a day, and ships are only able to enter and leave the dock in the period of about ninety minutes before and after high water. As a general rule, homeward bound trawlers dock on the flood, and those sailing leave on the ebb. Arrive five minutes after the gates have closed and you were stuck out at Wyre Light until the next tide. We liked to dock on the a.m. tide. It gave us an extra twelve hours in dock.

In the days before the National Dock Labour Board was formed we were expected to turn out to help unload the catch. Work started about 2.30 a.m. and finished about 7 a.m. We were paid twelve shillings for this service, but if we didn't turn up, twenty-four shillings was stopped off our pay, supposedly to pay for a replacement. I never did understand the logic of this arrangement.

After the fish was discharged the time was our

own until sailing time. The shore gang would take over and load the coal, ice, provisions, and deck and engineer's stores required for the next trip. The trawler would sail on the next early morning tide. A grand total of thirty-six hours in dock. I can recall times when I have gone home after landing the fish, so tired that I have gone to bed and slept like a log until being woke up at sailing time.

There was no such thing as paid holidays. If you wanted a break you signed off your ship, and your pay stopped until you signed on again. You couldn't draw the dole because you had left your employment.

When out of a ship there was one way we could earn a few bob. All the trawlers were armed with Lewis machine guns, and the bigger boats sported an Oerlikon anti-aircraft gun on the casing abaft the funnel. About ten o'clock every Monday morning a leading seaman from D.E.M.S. (Defensively Equipped Merchant Ships) Gunnery School in Dock Street would come down to the dock gates and round up as many unemployed trawlermen as he could muster to take part in a three day gunnery course. We were taught the rudiments of loading, firing, and looking after our weapons. On each of the three days we would move from the classroom to the Fleetwood Arms, the pub next door, to discuss tactics over a pint. The highlight of the course was a trip to the firing range on the last morning, where we all had a go at firing the guns. Although I attended this course several times I never quite got the hang of the technicalities. I could strip a Lewis gun, but when I tried to reassemble the implement I always had one or two bits left over. On completion of the course we received a Certificate stating that we were competent to operate these instruments of destruction, and paid thirty-six shillings. It was customary to drop the odd six bob in the begging bowl for the benefit of our naval instructors, which probably explains the zeal the leading seaman displayed in rounding up candidates for the course.

If the professional fighting men had treated their weapons in the slap happy way the trawlermen did I doubt if we would have won the war. Storage space was always at a premium, and when stowing up, it was common practice to store any odds and ends of loose gear in the Oerlikon turret. Had we ever needed the gun for its designed purpose it would have taken us half an hour to clear it. I only ever fired the Oerlikon once when at sea. We had been at anchor in Broad Bay sheltering from the weather, and the Old Man, probably sick of seeing us loafing about, ordered us to clean and oil the gun. The mate supervised the operation, and when finished, decided we'd fire a few bursts to ensure it was working. The Oerlikon is a big gun, and requires two men to cock and load it. The magazine weighs 56 pounds, and the half-inch shells are packed with tracer, armour piercing, and explosive projectiles in rotation. I was the guy that pulled the trigger. It's not much fun firing a gun without something to shoot at, and the only available targets were the seagulls wheeling round the ship. I didn't hit any of the birds, but I did knock the truck off the top of the after mast, and bring the aerials down.

One skipper I sailed under had a much more sensible and sedate approach to our weaponry. Skipper Laddie Bush was a veteran who hailed from Great Yarmouth. He was a gentleman to work for in every sense of the word. One trip, outward bound, we were steaming up Islay Sound. It was a pitch dark, clear night. I was at the helm, and Laddie was jammed up in the wing of the wheelhouse, making sure I didn't run his ship ashore. We heard the sound of an approaching aircraft which passed directly over us from the stern, and by the noise it was making it wasn't very high. A minute or two after it passed we heard the sound of its engines increase as it returned, and a searchlight beam from it lit up the wheelhouse.

"Shall I get the gun ready, Skipper?" I ventured, keen to display the skills I had half learned at the gunnery school. "No, Johnny," he said. "If its one of ours it doesn't matter. If its one of theirs it's good stokers I need, not good gunners."

At the time when the Germans were occupying Norway a group of Fleetwood ships were working off the south-east coast of Iceland. Every morning, about seven o'clock, a Foch Wulf four engined reconnaissance aircraft would pass over the ships, not much higher than the tops of the masts. Every evening, before tea, it would pass over the ships again on its return journey to some base in Norway. This aircraft never interfered with the trawlers, and the fishermen left well alone and ignored the plane. These long-range planes were used in the Atlantic as convoy spotters. Their tactics, on finding a convoy, was to circle the ships out of the range of gunfire, and broadcast the position, course, speed, and other details of the convoy to the lurking U-boat packs.

The general consensus among the trawlermen was that this particular aeroplane carried no armament. One morning one of the trawlers decided to put this opinion to the test, and opened up with the Oerlikon and Lewis guns at the low flying plane. The plane held its course apparently oblivious to this show of hostility. But later that day he dispelled the notion that he was unarmed. He returned half an hour earlier than was his usual practice, and coming in low out of the sun with machine guns blazing, he livened up the fishing, and blew away half the wheelhouse off his former attacker. After that incident, the status quo returned, each party ignoring the other. Life was unpleasant enough without further complications.

I spent two years as brassie, and a further year as deckhand, in the home water trawlers before I ventured to the fishing grounds at Iceland. Working around the Shetland, Orkney, and Western Isles, and off the coast of Ireland, fishing mainly for hake, with small crews, enabled me to learn every aspect of the work on deck. On those occasions when my ship was refitting I was found work in the net stores and rigging shop, and although the wage I was paid was a joke, the knowledge I acquired about a trawl, and the skills I was taught handling and splicing steel wires was invaluable.

I was a strong lad, with hands the size of dinner plates, and half as much sense as a horse; all the attributes to a career on the distant water trawlers. To complete my education I still had to experience the climatic conditions of the Arctic winter.

Chapter Three

THE HARD MEN

In a profession where hard men were as plentiful as the swallows in a decent summer, there was one who, for sheer brutality and ruthlessness in the way he treated his crews, stood head and shoulders above the other giants.

In Fleetwood, just before, and just after the war, Skipper Ernest (Ernie) Christy was a legend in his own lifetime.

I heard one old hand mutter, over a pint in the Strawberry bar "Do one trip with Christy and you're one of the boys. Do two trips and you're a hero. Do three and you're a bloody lunatic."

I sailed under his command in the Drusilla, one of J. Marr's ships, for four trips. I don't know what that makes me; what I do know is that afterwards, every other skipper I sailed under seemed a daddy in comparison. In those four trips he went through three mates, four bosuns, and four complete sets of deckhands. Don Rial, as good a mate as you were likely to find anywhere, was the man tough enough, foolish enough, or hard up enough, to stick him for two trips. Whether Ernie sacked him or not I don't know, but I did hear Don say to the ships husband at the end of the second trip "A voyage with Captain Blyth on the Bounty would seem like a holiday cruise after the last two trips."

At the time a rumour circulated round the docks

that Arty Marr had warned Christy "Better ease up a bit, Ernie, the war's making for a shortage of deck crews, and it's becoming easier to get a skipper than a deck crew."

What truth there is in that is a matter for conjecture, but if the Captain Christy I sailed under was a watered down version, then God help the poor sods that sailed with him in pre-war days when he was in full flight, and there was a plentiful supply of replacement crews.

One story I heard, and now repeat with tongue in cheek, concerns old Leggit and his horse. If Leggit had a first name I never heard it, but he was a well-known character on the fish docks.

Early in the war, all the empty fish boxes were moved from the box yard adjacent to the fish market to a field close to Rossal pumping station, and well away from the town, as a fire precaution in the event of air raids. Leggit and his old, grey mare earned some sort of a living carting the boxes down to the market every morning. One winter morning, when crossing the railway lines at the entrance to the docks, the horse slipped on the ice and fell across the railway lines, preventing the gates from closing, and halting the 0800 Liverpool train.

Sergeant Longsdale, of the Docks Police, and several bystanders, had been trying for half an hour to get the horse on its feet without success. Fred Dollin, Marr's ships husband, who had been watching the performance from the window of the Pool Office, strolled across.

"Want me to shift it for you, Sarge?", he said to the policeman.

"I wish you could, Fred," replied the man in blue, "but I don't see how."

Mr. Dollin crouched down beside the horse and whispered in its ear. Instantly the horse struggled to its feet and trotted off towards the fish market; old Leggit, taken by surprise, had to run to catch up. As Leggit, and horse and cart disappeared in the distance, Sergeant Longsdale regarded the ships husband in some awe. "What the hell did you say to it?" he asked.

"Oh" said Fred, with a grin "I told it Christy was docking on the tide and he wanted a full crew."

Whether or not you believe that story, it is a fact that the morning I signed on Drusilla, the Pool Office, the nearby teashop, and the area around the dock gates were deserted and the same phenomena was repeated every time Drusilla docked while I was in the ship, those fishermen with any sense keeping well away from the dock area, and Marr's office, until we were safely away at sea.

It wasn't that Skipper Christy was a loud man, always bawling and screaming out of the wheelhouse windows. In fact, he was just the opposite; the most taciturn, quietly spoken man I have ever met, but even his silence seemed to carry a threat. I don't think he uttered a dozen words a day while at sea. When he did speak, he only addressed one of two people, the mate or me, the apprentice, and then only to give an order.

On passage to the fishing grounds, he would come up to the wheelhouse, completely ignore any "Good morning, Skipper" the mate might offer, take an empty mug from the pot rack and wave it in the direction of the mate. The mate would then tell the decky on watch "Bring the Skipper a pot of tea." I don't think he ever got a mug that some member of the deck crew hadn't spat in.

Then Captain Christy would stare morosely out of the bridge window until the tea arrived, drink the tea amid an uneasy silence, and then disappear back to his lair. On the odd occasion he might say to the mate "Steer northwest", "watch the steering.", or maybe "call me at four." That would be his entire conversation for the day. Not one word wasted.

During fishing operations he was no different; hauling and shooting you never heard him. He expected the mate to know what was wanted, and left him to get on with it, although his eyes never left the deck while the men were working on it.

On hauling, if the trawl was so badly damaged it was quicker to change over, that is, shoot the gear on the other side, he simply stuck his head out of the window and indicated the other gear with a jerk of his head. Steaming to a new fishing ground, if he required a helmsman, I always got the job. Then he would extend his arm out of the window and beckon. A stranger could be forgiven for thinking he was dumb. When I arrived on the bridge, oilskins divested, and bearing two mugs of tea, he would take one of the proffered mugs, give me a course to steer, and resume staring out at the men working on deck, never saying another word.

While he didn't talk much, he didn't sleep much either, and he made sure no one else did.

The four trips I spent with him took place in the period from mid-October to December, a season when the weather around the Western Isles, where we were working, is not noted for its tranquility. Three of those trips were to St. Kilda, the most westerly of the islands.

From St. Kilda, the expanse of the Atlantic Ocean stretches westward, unbroken by land, the three thousand odd miles or so to the American eastern seaboard. Generated by gales spawned by the depressions that scurry eastward across this vast expanse of water, the white capped rollers, often as high as a three-story building, roar in like trains to pound the desolate, craggy cliffs and tors of the island. Between the frequent gales, the wind seldom drops below force 5 or 6, and on those rare days when it does, the next gale is with you before the swell has chance to die down.

The seabed surrounding the island is as rocky as the visible coastline. That means busted trawls. I'll guarantee from personal experience, that over an extended period, a brassie will fill more braiding needles and use more twine, and a decky will have sorer hands, when working at St. Kilda than when fishing on any other ground the Fleetwood ships worked.

The Fleetwood boats never worked a watch below. Fishing in home waters, Drusilla's deck complement consisted of mate, bosun, five deckhands, and a brassie; seven and a half men, just enough to work the gear efficiently.

I can't recall a single occasion when we pulled the gear aboard for weather. Sometimes, when pulling in the net, the ship laid broadside to the sea, the height of the waves would be frightening. A sea, it's white top higher than the masthead light, would come charging at you. The decky driving the winch would scream out "water," and the men at the ship's side would dash for the handrails that were welded all round the base of the wheelhouse about four feet above deck level, and hang on grimly. As the sea bore down on you the ship would rise on the swell, and you had the same feeling you get when going up in an elevator. At the top of the rise, as the ship rolled into the wind, the white top of the roller would curl over the bulwarks, filling the deck to the top of the rail. All you could do, chest deep in icy water, would be to cling to the handrail, and try to stay on your feet. As the ship rolled the other way the water would pour across the duck pond, and out of the scuppers the other side, leaving behind three or four seagulls, which had been washed aboard, trying frantically to get airborne, and half a dozen cursing fishermen, half blinded by salty spray, and soaked through to the skin. One curse I heard often that winter was "He'll lose this bastard before he's finished," but mercifully he never did. There is a limit to how many changes of clothes you can take to sea with you. I used to take four sets, and more than once the gear I was wearing would be saturated, and the other three sets hung up to dry.

On the St. Kilda fishing ground the daily work pattern was always the same. We shot the gear about six o'clock in the morning, trawled all day, and hauled the gear for the last time about midnight, the net then staying aboard until six the next morning. The five or six hours break from towing the gear was not a concession to tired eyes and aching muscles. It was a necessity. The best fishing was in the deep water during the daytime, so when the gear was busted, which was most hauls, the tattered net was botched together as quickly as possible so as to lose as little of the daylight fishing as practical. As a result, after the last haul there were two trawls to overhaul and renew before the next day's fishing started.

With most skippers the crew concentrated their efforts on the starboard gear, and as soon as the work on it was completed half the men would turn in for two or three hours until they were required for shooting. The other half would start work on the port gear. After shooting the trawl, the men that had been on deck all night would turn in until hauling time, their mates finishing the work on the port trawl. With that system everyone got a couple of hours sleep each day.

But that was too easy for Captain Christy. Aboard Drusilla all hands stayed up until the work on both gears was finished, and by then it was time to start fishing again, with the result that you were lucky to get a couple of hours kip every other day. As the apprentice I avoided this ordeal. After the last haul of fish was gutted, as soon as all my needles were full, the mate ordered me to turn in till shooting time, so I always got five hours sleep a day.

It wasn't the trips at St. Kilda, hard as they were, that put Christy at the top of my list of hard men. I've no doubt that many trawlermen can re- count similar experiences. The last time I had the dubious honour of sailing under him took place during the first fortnight in December. We were working at the top end of the Minch, on the east side between Ru Stoer and Ru Rea. All the time we had been on the ground the weather had been lousy, a westerly near gale force wind that drove the smaller ships to the sheltered anchorages in Broad Bay or Loch Eribol, and the bigger boats to scratch a living in the more sheltered water under the lee of Tiumpan Head. We stayed put the whole time, swilled about, and never off the deck. At the end of eight day's work we had close to a thousand kits of dogfish down the fishroom.

If that doesn't seem a lot of fish to the East Coast deep water men, remember that there were only seven men on deck; we were working two gears on hard ground, and in the Fleetwood ships, where everything was done the hard way, all the dogs had to be gutted. Then the generators packed up, and without any deck lights, and oil navigation lights rigged, we crossed the Minch to Stornaway for re- pairs.

For the benefit of those of you strange to com- mercial fishing, the dogfish is pretty obnoxious to handle in bulk. Its skin is like course sandpaper, and after a couple of hauls gutting, the skin on your fingers begins to wear away, a condition that gets steadily worse as the trip progresses. The only rem- edy is to stop gutting dogs. To compound matters, the dogfish has a needle sharp spike at the back of its dorsal fin that inflicts painful punctures to hands and wrists that very soon fester. So, after gutting a thousand kits of dogs, splicing the warps three or four times, and mending and pulling two sets of gear about for eight days, our hands were in a bad state; so sore it was an agony trying to undo the buttons on your fearnought flaps when you wanted a piss.

Apart from the discomfort caused by sore hands, there was the tiredness. For eight days the men had averaged no more than three hours sleep a day. Not three hours continuous sleep, but sleep snatched in cat naps, and they were almost out on their feet. In this respect, I had come off better, being allowed to turn in from about 11 p.m. till 6 a.m., just being called out to haul and shoot, so most nights I was enjoying the luxury of five or six hours off the deck, split into two periods.

Throughout the last day's fishing the wind had increased steadily, and by the time we had scrambled the gear aboard and lashed it up, and the trawl doors were stowed inboard, it was gusting up to force 10. Pounding against a head wind and sea, the steam to Stornaway, about thirty odd miles, took about eight hours. It being impossible to work on deck without lights in the existing weather conditions, two steaming watches were set, and all hands got a welcome four hours in their bunks.

We entered Stornaway harbour and tied up to the east side of Number 2 Pier at about four in the morning. As soon as the ropes were made fast, despite the fact that we had no deck lights, Christy wanted his trawls overhauling. With the illumination provided by a couple of paraffin anchor lanterns, the work was completed by seven o'clock. Just after breakfast, the shore engineers having inspected the generators, word filtered through to the deck crew that the repairs would not be completed for another twenty-four hours. The Old Man was seen

through his porthole having a shave, a sure sign that when we left Stornaway we would be going home. There was a good trip of fish down the fishroom, and despite the fact that we still had to endure the misery imposed by the skipper for another three days, we were all in a buoyant mood. The fishing was finished, we were convinced, and soon we'd be back in Fleetwood.

As opening time approached the lads started to drift down the quay in the direction of the bars that front the harbour. No one turned up for dinner. Too bad if they had; the cook was down at the pub as well. Before the mate had gone ashore he'd ordered, "Give the wheelhouse a birthday, Johnny, and I want to be able to see my face in the brass when I go up there."

I had just finished polishing the brasswork when the Old Man entered the bridge. Handing me a pound note, "Nip up the road and get me three or four bottles of beer," he said.

Donning my duffle coat, I then strolled towards the town. After a leisurely walk along the quays, I purchased six bottles of beer at the Caledonian Hotel, sipped a Vimto and chatted up the wee lassie serving in the snack bar half way along South Beach, then made my way back to the ship.

When I arrived back, either the bars had closed, or the crew's money had evaporated, because all the deck crew were grouped on the quay, laughing and joking noisily in the way a bunch of drunks will.

"What's in the bag, Snacker?" the mate said to me, eyeing the carrier I was carrying.

"Some beer for the Old Man." I replied.

"It's not beer that bastard needs," he said, and

taking the carrier from me added, "he owes us a drink anyway."

Then, with an air of alcohol induced bravado, he proceeded to hand out the beer. "Only six, you and Harry will have to share one," he said to one of the trimmers.

"There'll be hell to pay if he doesn't get his beer. He'll go mad," I protested.

"Don't worry, Kiddo," said the bosun with a grin, "If he goes mad we'll have to shoot him." And with that they all sat on the edge of the jetty, legs dangling over the choppy water of the harbour, and proceeded to demolish Christy's ale.

Me, I was cold sober. I knew there was going to be trouble. What form that trouble would take I couldn't imagine, but come it would, as inevitable as night follows day. I slipped aboard and concealed myself down the fo'c'sle, harbouring the crazy idea that if I kept out of sight long enough the skipper might forget his beer.

By about four o'clock hunger drove me from my hiding place. The other occupants of the fo'c'sle were sleeping off the effects of their run ashore, and it was just starting to go dark. I made my way aft, made myself a sandwich, and with a mug of tea in one hand, and a cheese banjo in the other, stepped out on to the deck to nearly collide with the Old Man.

"Where's my beer?," he said.

Taken by surprise I could only blurt out "The mate's had it, Skipper." I expected him to explode, but it didn't happen. In fact, he didn't show any emotion at all, just "tell the Chief Engineer I want him on the bridge."

I found the Chief working on his engine.

"The Old Man wants you on the bridge, chief." I said.

"Know what for, Son?" he asked.

"No, but I think its trouble, chief. He's not in a very good mood." I answered.

"Is he ever?" he said, wiping his hands on a lump of cotton waste, and making for the engine room ladder.

I followed him up the ladder, then remembering I still had a couple of shillings change from the Skipper's pound note, and curious to know what was afoot, trailed up to the bridge.

Captain Christy met the chief at the wheelhouse door.

"I'm not waiting for the generators. Be ready to sail at six. Rig up four gas lights; one over the towing block, one each side under the veranda, and one on the foredeck, and make sure they won't blow away."

"There's not much time if you're sailing at six, Skipper." complained the chief.

"No" agreed Christy, "So you'd better get a move on or you'll be doing it in the weather", and with that the bridge door closed, leaving a chief engineer muttering inaudible curses, and an apprentice holding a half-eaten banjo in one hand, and a few coppers in the other. Judgement Day was fast approaching.

We left Stornaway at 1800 hours with the generators still unserviceable, and three hours later we stopped to shoot on Scrobie Bank. The weather had been very bad when we had arrived at the port; it wasn't much better when we left. We had no deck lights, and I was armed with a torch made from a yard length of stiff wire with a lump of paraffin-soaked cotton waste tied to one end with seizing wire. My job, during the dark hours, was to go round lighting the carbide gas lights all the time the gear was being hauled and shot. I'd light the one over the towing block aft, then work my way for'ard. By the time I'd lit the light over the foredeck all the others had blown out, so I'd make my way aft and start again.

After towing only an hour we hauled, and I played the lamplighter again. There was no fish, but the net was in tatters. As soon as the damaged trawl had been pulled aboard the Old Man beckoned me up to the wheelhouse, gave me a course to steer, and jammed himself in the starboard wing, from where he could keep an eye on the men working on the deck. As we proceeded south at slow speed, wind and sea were just abaft the beam, and periodically I could hear the water crashing aboard over the men trying to mend the net on the weather side.

Repairs to the net were completed about midnight, and immediately Christy stopped to shoot, and I had to do my lamp-lighting act again. This time we had only been towing twenty minutes when the gear came fast on an obstruction, and when we heaved it back on board the net was again in tatters. I was told to turn in for the night, just being called out to play the lamp lighter when the gear was being hauled and shot, but there was no respite for the rest of the men. They were out on deck in the weather all night.

When I was called out at breakfast time the weather had moderated quite a bit. Both wind and sea had dropped considerably, and this made for more comfortable working conditions, but now the skipper started to use both gears, paralysing first one, and then the other, so that whether steaming or towing there was always at least one trawl that required mending.

And so it went on. It was obvious by now that the skipper wasn't trying to catch fish. He was extracting payment for his six bottles of beer, and if ever an exorbitant price was paid, those men on deck paid it.

Between Scrobie Bank and Wyre Dock there are numerous patches of foul ground, and Christy knew every one of them. From leaving Stornaway to passing Wyre Light we took three and a half days, from Wednesday evening till Sunday morning, and during the whole of that time the men were never off the deck except for the half hour break at meal times. I saw one man fall asleep at dinner, and his head fell in his soup plate. We used up every ball of twine aboard the ship, the men were nearly out on their feet, and since leaving Stornaway we hadn't put one fish down the fishroom. They were still mending the net as we approached the locks, and by now their hands looked like slices of raw meat. I'd had it relatively easy. I was turning in every night from midnight till breakfast time, and for most of the rest of the time was helmsman.

We tied up stem on to the fish market, and Skipper Christy rang "Finished With Engines" on the telegraph. If he was tired it didn't show. As the last mooring rope was made fast he called out to the mate "Sweep that manure off the fo's'le head", referring to the crew, and watched a very subdued bunch of men descend the ladder from the whaleback, men too exhausted even to curse.

Looking back, I suppose the men could have decided enough was enough and threw their hand in, but these men were hard, very experienced seamen. They knew the score. Under the archaic laws that regulate the lives of all seamen, a ship's master stands next to God, and a seaman who refuses to obey a lawful command is regarded as a criminal, and treated as such. Had they refused to work collectively, this would have been construed as mutiny. As a consequence, when the ship arrived in port they would have been hauled before a court, in all probability the presiding magistrate having family or business connections with the shipowner, and heavily fined. The fine imposed would have taken care of that trip's remuneration, but would not have constituted the total penalty. Subsequent to the court proceedings, the men would have been spragged, that is, they would have been blacklisted, and unable to find work on any other trawler until such time as the owners considered they had learned their lesson.

In this particular instance, most of the men had families to support, and Christmas was just round the corner. They needed the money, so were in a no win situation.

That was my last trip with Skipper Christy. When I came down to the Pool Office on landing day I was surprised to find it was crowded. I soon discovered why. Eddie Chard was the ships husband presiding over the log books that morning. "Your Uncle Ernie is changing over to the Dinorah, and he's left word you'll be going with him, John, so come down on Thursday morning to sign on," he said good-humouredly. The Drusilla, without Skipper Christy, was a good money-earning ship to be in. Word had gone round about the change of command, and that explained the crowd. I left the office pretending not to notice the admiring glances from the two or three brassies, and the sympathetic ones from the older hands.

On each of the last four trips I'd had a good pay off, and I'd saved a few bob. It was time to have a holiday. On Thursday I was the missing link, and I kept out of sight until the Dinorah was well out at sea. In another week there would be the usual shortfall of labour as men stayed at home for Christmas and New Year. It wouldn't be difficult to get a berth in a good ship, especially for a lad who had completed four trips with Skipper Ernest Christy. In those days a man was evaluated according to the class of ships he'd sailed in, and the length of time he'd stayed in them.

But, although I never realized it at the time, I learned a great deal in those four trips, and owe a debt of gratitude to the men I sailed with during them, especially to Skipper Christy who demonstrated, in no uncertain terms, what commanding a trawler is all about. All the men from the mates to the bosun helped turn me into a better trawlerman, and I'm a better man from having known them.

Chapter Four

THE MAN IN THE BOAT

The episode of the Man In The Boat took place in the summer of 1942, and was witnessed by two people. From start to finish, the macabre spectacle lasted maybe five minutes at most, but made a lasting impression on at least one of the observers, if not both.

To the elder of the two, a seasoned mariner who had traversed all of the seven seas more than once, the event again emphasized a fact demonstrated to him on more than one previous occasion: no matter how many years you spend afloat, the sea always has one or two nasty surprises to throw at you, and does so when you least expect them.

To the younger of the two, a boy on the threshold of manhood and a lifetime at sea, it brought the realization that there is more to warfare than gunfire, beating drums, and waving banners, and that there are many ways of dying at sea.

––––––––––––

Skipper Charles Hargrieves, Lt. Commander R.N.R. (Retired), 62 years old next Friday, was a contented man. For once, the weather had been kind.

Ten days ago he had manoeuvered the Springwell away from her berth opposite the elevator in Wyre Dock, and passed through the locks into the River Wyre.

It had been a fine, sunny morning. His wife, Hilda, had been in her usual place, at the end of Jubilee Quay, just clear of the stern of the Isle of Man boat, to wave him off, and he had stepped out on to the port veranda to return the wave. How often had that farewell gesture been repeated the last thirty-odd years?

The passage across Morcambe Bay, through North Channel, and the run off to St. Kilda had been equally placid. For eight days the Springwell had trawled along the edge of the deep water southwest of the island, and not a breath of wind the whole time. The fishing had been good, too. True, for the last five days they'd been plagued with fog with visibility seldom more than a cable, but he could put up with that. You couldn't have everything.

He plucked the mug from the rack, took a deep swig at the tea it contained, replaced the mug, and studied the fish tally the mate had given him at breakfast. They had a good trip in. The tally said 550 kits, mostly hake. They'd have a bit more than that. Olly's tallies were always on the conservative side. On and off they'd been together five, maybe nearer six, years, and he couldn't recall a single trip that they hadn't landed forty or fifty boxes more than the tally. This trip would be no different. If their luck held he planned to dock on the Thursday p.m. tide, land the fish for Friday's market, and sail on the Monday. It was time they had a weekend in port; both men and ship could do with it. It would give the shore fitters time to do some work on the heap of scrap below deck that they had the audacity to call an engine. The whole ship would have been converted to razor blades before now but for the start of the bloody war. But there were ships in worse condition plying the sea lanes - much worse. Assuming the weather held, and that was anybody's guess, docking Thursday left them with two more days to put the icing on the cake. Things looked good, though it didn't do to plan too far ahead; not on this job. There were over three hundred miles of water separating them from the fish dock at Fleetwood. Anything could happen, and probably would.

Friday was his birthday, and if he knew Hilda she'd be planning a little celebration; a family get-together, at least, a get-together of those who weren't away at the war. They had been married 37 years now and he'd never regretted one minute of it. Like any other couple, they'd had their ups and downs. Possibly the worst time was during the coal strike in 1926. Nearly all the ships were laid up. There was no coal to run them. He'd given his gold watch and chain to Hilda to take to Uncles, the pawn shop on the corner of Mount Street and Lord Street, almost opposite Tommy Ball's clog shop. The proceeds allowed them to eat for two months. He'd been able to redeem it later in the year, and still had it. In 1926 Thompson's pledge office was probably the busiest shop in Fleetwood.

He never did get his D.S.O. back, nor did he want to. He'd flogged it to a dealer in Talbot Road, Blackpool, for three quid. He hadn't earned it anyway, although the local paper made a bit of a fuss about it at the time. Hilda still had the press cuttings stowed carefully away with the birth certificates, marriage lines, and insurance policies in the tin at the bottom of the wardrobe.

He smiled wryly as his mind went back to the events that led up to that night in the autumn of 1917. They had been part of an escort group nursing a convoy of merchant ships bound for Malta, as far as Gibraltar. From the time they passed Ushant to the time they hove to under the Rock they'd had little respite. It seemed that every U-Boat in the Atlantic was concentrated along that stretch of water. They had lost three of the merchant ships, and he had fished thirty-four survivors out of the water. Every man on board was dog-tired, but it was over now, at least for the time being. They would get a couple of days rest, perhaps even a jaunt ashore on the liberty boat.

It didn't work out like that though.

Almost before the ship had swung to her anchor the orders had come from ashore.

"Take bunkers and stores forthwith stop After bunkering proceed to Liverpool post-haste, repeat, post-haste."

It had been an all-hands job to bunker and store, and eight hours later, with the seamen still swilling away the coal dust that clung to the deck fittings and the sides of the superstructure with the tenacity that shit clings to a blanket, he had edged the boat away from the bunkering berth and pointed her head seaward. An Aldis lamp flickered on one of the sweepers anchored off the south end of the boom.

The young signalman perched in the wing of the bridge scribbled on his pad and handed him the message: "Goodbye my Love."

"Tell him bollocks," he had snarled, and rang Full Ahead with a savagery that surprised the other occupants of the bridge. The Aldis lamp resumed its clicking, the bow wave surged up from the raked stem as engine revolutions built up, and they headed back to the war. If they had been dog-tired when they arrived at Gibraltar, they were completely knackered when they left.

Night closed round them. The drizzle that had persisted all afternoon had turned into a downpour. He felt the throb of the engines through the soles of his boots, heard the displaced water hissing along the ship's sides, ignored the rivulets of rainwater racing each other down the outside of the weather shield, his eyes fixed ahead, trying in vain to pierce the wall of blackness ahead of them. By God, he was tired. The whole ship's company was tired. Somewhere out there were the U-Boats. He wondered if they were tired too. But they wouldn't be fighting each other tonight. They could pass within half a cable and be ignorant of each others presence in these conditions.

Without taking his eyes from the darkness ahead, "Number One."

"Sir." He felt, rather than saw, the tall skinny figure of the first officer emerge from the curtain screening the asdic compartment.

"Go and put your feet up for a couple of hours. I'll call you if I need you."

"I'm O.K. Sir."

He turned to face the figure outlined in the faint glow of light thrown out by the binnacle lamp.

"Do it, Number One, tomorrow might be a busy day."

"Aye, Aye, Sir," he had made his half-protest, and you didn't argue with the Old Man when he addressed you in that tone.

The Old Man heard the clump of boots on the ladder, the clang and rattle as the storm door closed and the dogs were secured; turned to face the wall of darkness ahead and resumed his vigil.

Lieutenant Antony Walsh had been with him two years now, he reflected. Wouldn't be long before they gave him a ship of his own, what, with all the new boats coming from the yards, and the number of men they were losing. It must be a full time job sending all those telegrams out "The Admiralty regrets to inform you ...." He didn't go much on that. Not that Tony didn't deserve the chance. God knows, he'd earned it, and Charlie Hargrieves wouldn't stand in his way. But then he'd have the hassle of breaking in his successor. As if he didn't have enough to do. His mind leaped back to their first meeting.

They were in the final stages of commissioning the Wolverine. He hadn't moved aboard yet - that could wait until the rest of the crew arrived. Hilda had come up for the week, and they were billeted at the County, the small hotel across the road from the yard gates. Sat at the desk in the corrugated iron shed across from the Wolverine's berth, he listened to rain hammering on the tin roof and surveyed the piles of paper littering the desk top with distaste. The sub, who should have been sorting out the paperwork in front of him, had been carted off to hospital, suspected ulcers, and his replacement hadn't arrived yet.

His thoughts were interrupted by the knock on the door.

"Come in."

The door creaked open and a blast of cold Clydeside air scattered the papers on the desk.

"Close the bloody door before we all get pneumonia."

The door closed and he appraised the tall, slightly built youth standing stiffly in front of the desk.

"Sub L'tenant Walsh reporting to H.M.S. Wolverine, Sir."

"Been to sea before, sub?" he enquired, but knowing the answer.

"A spot of yachting on the Solent and a long weekend on the trainer at Dartmouth, Sir. The Wolverine's my first real ship. I've been aboard and they told me I'd find you here."

"Good. We're not working a ship's routine yet. No point till we have enough people to fill the slots. Get yourself aboard, have a good look round, and get to know your way about. The coxun'll fix you up with a boiler suit; you'll need it. We'll be having lunch in the P.O.'s mess. The ward room's not open yet. After lunch you can come back here and start on this lot." He indicated the piles of paper with a nod of his head.

"Yes, Sir," The boy saluted again and turned for the door.

"Oh, and sub, you don't salute me when I'm not wearing my cap."

Another blast of cold air, and Sublieutenant Antony Walsh R.N.V.R., apprehensive in a new environment, desperately anxious to please, forced his way through the driving rain to the shelter that was Wolverine.

That was two years ago. Two years of war that had transformed the callow youth, still wet behind the ears, with a boyish grin, a degree in economics, and a sheltered, middle class upbringing, into the confidently efficient professional seaman he was today.

"Cocoa, Sir."

"Thank you," he took the steaming mug from the young seaman.

"The coxon's put a tot of rum in it, Sir." "Good man. Tell him I'll return the compliment when I see him in the Bowling Green."

"The Bowling Green, Sir?"

"He'll know."

He moved into the shelter of the darkened chart room, sat down on the locker, and drained the mug in one long swig. He lit a cigarette and felt the cocoa he had drunk warming his guts. The heat from the bulkhead radiator crept over him, eyelids heavy as lead weights closed over tired eyes, and the half-smoked cigarette slipped from his fingers.

Twenty miles sou'west of Faro, U 29 laid on the surface charging the batteries that were so essential if she were to continue to operate as a fighting unit. The night was black as pitch, and the rain came down in sheets. Ideal conditions for her purpose, but extremely uncomfortable for the watchman, who huddled in the conning tower, trying without much success to find shelter from the downpour. Two more hours and he'd be relieved. It was ten weeks since they'd left their pen at Bremerhaven and soon they'd be heading back home. They had only two torpedoes left. Maybe they could fire them tomorrow. . . .

The sudden lurch threw him off the locker, his arm hitting the corner of the chart table, knocking the skin off his elbow. Instantly awake, he tried to identify the sound of tortured metal tearing under the stress of impact.

Torpedo. No, no explosion.

Aground. Impossible, the nearest land was over twenty miles away.

Floating wreckage. Probably, there was plenty of it about.

The various alternatives raced through his mind in the seconds it took him to reach the front of the bridge.

The searchlight beam cut through the darkness, and he saw the U-Boat. They had hit her on the port side, just fore side the conning tower, nearly cutting her in half. The bow was still embedded in her belly, it seemed. Like a sausage on the end of a fork, he thought.

"Slow astern."

"Helm amidships."

"Ring action stations."

"Port twenty."

"Stop engines."

The commands were automatic, and as Wolverine settled broadside to the stricken submarine he saw the hole in her side, big as a garage door, and heard the torrent of water pouring through the gap. Saw the figure descending the ladder down the side of the conning tower slip, bounce on the steel deck, and roll into the water. There was no need for action stations; it was over in minutes. As the forward compartments flooded her stern towered out of the water, and she slid under. The sea boiled white as the air was squeezed out of her, and as the bubbles subsided a rapidly spreading oil slick was all that remained of U 29. All hands had got three weeks leave while the crumpled stem had been rebuilt. He'd been awarded a D.S.C..

Amazing. You steam over twenty thousand miles in hostile waters. Put in countless sleepless nights on the bridge. Sweep and destroy hundreds of mines, and pick up a couple of hundred survivors from blazing ships, and not even a thank you, except maybe from the poor bastards you pull from the drink, more dead than alive. One night you bob off for ten minutes when you should be awake and they give you a bloody medal.

His mind returned to the party he knew Hilda would be planning.

Richard had phoned to say he'd probably be able to get home that weekend. He was proud of that lad, now a full-blown lieutenant, and in the process of fitting out one of the new corvettes at Barrow. Over two hundred foot long and specially designed for antisubmarine warfare, Dick had told him. When you come to think of it hunting submarines is pretty much the same as hunting fish. The only difference is that the submarines can bite back.

He couldn't see his other lads getting home; both were somewhere at sea.

When the war broke out all three lads had flocked, with all the other idiots, to enlist. Just like he'd been an idiot in the last shindy; just like he'd nearly been an idiot in this one. Too old for sea service they'd told him, but he could do a good job at one of the training establishments, maybe the Sparrows

Nest. He shuddered at the thought. Signing chits and checking store lists all day. Sipping pink gins and patting the arses of the young, and not so young, wrens at the endless round of wardroom parties with the bunch of lounge lizards who wore the uniform with such elegance, never seemed to go to sea, and appeared as if by magic in the wardroom of any docking ship almost before the mooring ropes had been made fast, to claim their ration of free gin, and scrounge their quota of duty frees. O.K. for some, but not his cup of tea. He had declined the offer, preferring to do his bit at sea on the trawlers.

Betty would be there with the kids; he smiled when he thought of her. She'd always been his favourite. Born seven years after the youngest of the lads, the daughter they had always wanted, but despaired of ever having, had been spoiled rotten. Disinclined to send their darling Betty to St. Mary's, the Roman Catholic school the boys had attended, they had scraped together the fees for her to be educated at the Stella Maris Convent as a day girl. After completing her education, with the connivance of Dr. Cotton, the parish priest, she had found work teaching at the local Catholic kindergarten, a fitting occupation for the refined young lady she now was. Most of the Fleetwood lassies at that time worked, if they were lucky enough to have a job, at one of the fish houses that were situated along the Cops, or as net braiders at the Gourock works, or one of the other net making establishments in the Dock Street area, where besides sweating their arses off for bare subsistence wages, they learned a vocabulary strong enough to rival that of the young trawlermen they courted, used it with fluency when at work or with

their own gender, but feigned shock and innocence when within earshot of the same profanity when in the company of their boy friends.

He received quite a surprise when, after docking one Sunday morning, he was told, "Put on a tie for tea. Betty's boyfriend is coming round." He didn't know she had a boyfriend. He took fresh stock of her and for the first time it dawned on him that his baby was no longer a child, but an attractive young woman, quite a dishy young woman at that.

It was a bigger surprise when, later that evening, Hilda confided in him that the wedding had been arranged at St. Mary's in three weeks time; the banns had already been read out.

After the initial feelings of anger and indignation had subsided, he found he quite liked the look of his future son-in-law. Harry Walmsley, the son of a local jobbing builder, had served his time as a bricklayer in his father's business. A well built young man, he had the callused hands of a worker, a firm handshake, and looked you straight in the face when he spoke to you.

"Don't worry, Mr. Hargrieves," the lad had said, "I'll look after her."

For a wedding present he had given them the down payment on the small Edwardian terrace house in Radcliffe Road, just a stones throw from Ash Street tram stop. Six months to the day after the wedding Betty gave birth to his grandson. Eighteen months later she gave birth to her second child, a girl. Then the war came, and Harry was called up for the army. Now a sergeant in the Royal Engineers, he had been away over a year. Hilda had wanted Bet and the kids to move in with them for the duration; there was plenty of room in the rambling house they had in Seabank Road, but Betty had been adamant.

"No, Mum", she said with a finality they had to accept, "when Harry comes home he'll expect a home to come to, and I'll be there to welcome him."

He checked the water on the sounder and glanced at the clock. Still half an hour to hauling time. He continued to stare ahead into the fog that enveloped them; at the spot on the starboard bow where he thought he had seen a small patch a bit darker than its surroundings. There was nothing there now though; eyes can play queer tricks in fog, he thought. He imagined he saw the dark patch again. "There is something there," he muttered, and altered course a couple of points to starboard. After steadying the boat on her new course, he took the binoculars from the case hanging on the engine-room voice pipe, and stepped out on to the veranda.

As he trained the glasses on the darkening patch, the ship's gentle roll to port caused the wheelhouse door to slam shut with a metallic clang.

Johnny was a big lad for his age. Just sixteen years old, he had been fishing a little over a year now, and this was his sixth trip on the Springwell. Being a strong lad and not frightened of hard work, he got on well with the crew, who, when they weren't working or sleeping, impressed him with stories of the physical prowess, and fish catching ability of mates and skippers of yesteryears. The tales always started the same; "I remember one trip in the ...." His father, a prominent trawlerman, now serving in the navy, often featured in these stories. Sometimes, usually after he had made a

cock up of some job, the bosun or one of the deckies would survey his handiwork and comment, with just a touch of rancour, "You've made a right balls of that, Johnny. You'll never be as good as your old man. I remember one trip ....," and he would settle down to listen, with some pride, to an account of some spectacular activity in which his father had played a leading roll. He was proud of his dad.

The old hands were prepared to teach him the job, and he was a willing and enthusiastic pupil. Already he could steer the ship and box the compass; he knew what was expected of him when the trawl was being hauled and shot without having to be told every time, and he could gut fish nearly as fast as the deckies. Mending the trawl was the hardest aspect of the job to learn. Not braiding in the small tears in the net. Tommy had taught him that on the piece of old net he had pegged out under the whaleback, and on which he practiced when he had the time, and his hands weren't too sore. The difficult part was when the trawl came aboard in a tangled mass of rags and tatters, to sort out the mess, and recognize when and where new net needed to be shot in. He never had to actually help with this job. He was always too busy at the needle basket, filling and handing out the braiding needles, and collecting the empties for refilling. He could only watch and admire from a distance, the artistry of the mate and bosun, as they brought order to chaos in no time at all, and seemed to know what was needed almost before the tattered remnants of the trawl had been pulled aboard.

The skipper had promised him that the next time Springwell had a refit he would try to arrange for him to work with the shore gang until the ship was ready for sea, half the time in the net stores, the other half in the rigging shop.

"Then we'll think about giving you a start decky. No reason why you shouldn't make a good bosun one day, you've got all the necessary qualities," he'd said. He then demolished any ego the half compliment may have aroused in his young apprentice by adding laconically "You're as strong as a horse, and have half as much sense."

Old Grievsie wasn't a bad bloke, though, he thought. Do your work and you were O.K. Like all the other top skippers, he was a ruthless old bastard, and worked your bollocks off. He fished in some queer weather too. Johnny recalled that late afternoon a couple of trips ago. They had arrived at the fishing ground to the west of the Faroes, and Olly had called the Old Man twenty minutes before they reached the position marked on the chart. To say the weather was lousy would have been the understatement of the year. A nor'west wind gusting between force 8 and 9 on the Beaufort Scale, driving rain and sleet punctuated with short but frequent hail squalls, seas like mountains, their white tops breaking over the fo'c'sle head every few minutes, the resultant spray lashing the front of the wheelhouse and threatening to stove the windows in, and Springwell pitching and rolling her guts out.

Grievsie had come up to the bridge rubbing the sleep out of his eyes, opened the lee side door, and with knees jammed against the sides of the door frame to counter the ship's motion had urinated over the edge of the veranda into the scuppers ten feet below. The call of nature satisfied he had closed the door, checked the depth of water on the echosounder, and said to the mate, "Bring her round and stop her on the starboard tack, Olly."

The manoeuvre completed, Springwell rolled and wallowed in the trough of the seas like a turd in a piss pot.

Dropping the weather window, he poked his head out, and stared into the tempest for a full ten minutes, carefully assessing the violence of wind and sea. Apparently satisfied, he slammed the window up, turned, and to no one in particular muttered, "It's going to be a wild night. Not fit to turn a dog out.", and in almost the same breath "Call the lads out to shoot, Johnny, before they get bed sores."

When he, Johnny, had got to the fo'c'sle to impart the news with the customary "Down trawl" the reception he got was both ill-tempered and predictable.

"In this weather. You're joking, kid."

"The stormy bastard."

"Webbed feet, that's what you need in this cow."

"He must think we're bloody divers."

It might be as well to mention here that a very fine line, and a considerable grey area, divides what is workable weather and what is not. Wind and sea are not the only components the skipper must consider. The sea-kindliness and engine power of the ship must be allowed for. The nature of the ground to be trawled over, clear or foul, can be a deciding factor. The skipper's own ability, and the skill of the men working on deck, make a difference. What are merely unpleasant and highly dangerous conditions for one crew can be suicidal with a less experienced team. The final variable in the equation, rarely discussed, is the return steaming time to the nearest medical facilities in the event of a man being seriously injured. Getting this calculation right, at least most of the time, is one of the attributes that separates the top skippers from the rest of the herd. Competition at the top was so keen that you had to push ship and men to, and beyond, their limits of endurance if you were to stay at the top of the pack.

But the weather wasn't bad now. As the ship rolled gently in the slight Atlantic swell that never seemed to die down completely, and chugged through the clammy fog that enveloped her like a shroud, it seemed to Johnny that they were the only ship on the ocean; that here, somewhere off the Western Isles, they were in a world of their own, populated only by themselves and the few seagulls that glided in and out of the mist, or sat on the water preening themselves, and seeming oblivious of the trawler passing only a few yards from them.

Sat on the bits on the starboard quarter, from where he could see the marks on the trawl warps, he was peeling prawns to take home, a basket of whole crustaceans between his knees, and a new liver basket alongside him into which he was dropping the finished product. Already he had cleaned three baskets full, one each for the skipper, mate, and bosun, and he had two more to do. One basket for Tommy, the decky who would boil them all during the night watch after the cook had vacated the galley, the other for himself. His Mum liked prawns. He wondered if Betty liked them. He would take her a few anyway.

He thought about Betty, and felt himself going hard. He had met her on landing day at the end of his first trip in Springwell.

When the ship docked all the crew, except for the skipper, had to report to the ship at 0200 hours to help with unloading the catch, a job that occupied them till about 0730. After the work was finished Johnny had to deliver a parcel of some of the best fish in the catch to the skipper's house, a service for which the Old Man always gave him ten bob, or, on one or two occasions when they had made an exceptionally good trip, a pound.

When he arrived at the big house in Seabank Road, Mrs. Hargrieves invariably welcomed him with, "You look tired, luv, come in and have a cup of tea.", an invitation he gratefully accepted. As he sat at the deal table in the kitchen, sipping a mug of scalding, sickly sweet tea, she would keep up an incessant flow of conversation.

"Was it a hard trip?"

"What's the weather been like?"

"How is your mother, John. I haven't seen her for ages."

"Isn't it time your father was home on leave? It'll be a happy day when this hideous war finishes and we can settle down to normality again."

On his first visit to the house, after the initial flow of pleasantries had been completed, she had said "Dear me, I really don't know what I'm going to do today. I usually take Betty, that's our daughter, a bit of fish, but we have a committee meeting this afternoon over at Mrs. Leadbetters, and I simply must be there." She was secretary of the local branch of the W.V.S..

"I don't know why Charles had to pick today to land. Men are so inconsiderate."

"I could take it round for you, Mrs. Hargrieves," he'd replied, not really wanting to, but not knowing what else to say.

"Would you. That would be wonderful. You are a darling," she had enthused.

So Johnny had left with armed with a bag of fish, an address in Radcliffe Road, and "Be sure to give my regards to your Mum, and tell her to pop round before too long." ringing in his ears.

He hadn't delivered the fish straight away. He'd gone home, had breakfast and a bath, then feeling the effects of twenty-four hours without sleep, had laid down on his bed. It was close to noon when he awoke.

Dressing hurriedly, he then made his way to the company office to draw his pay for the trip. He left the office, with twenty pounds or so safely stowed in his hip pocket and feeling like a millionaire, to spend the afternoon playing snooker at Holts, the billiard hall in Preston Street, and swapping suitably embroidered sea stories with the other young fishermen that frequented the place. He was at home having his tea before he remembered the parcel of fish he had to deliver.

It was almost eight o'clock that evening when he tapped on the door of the house in Radcliffe Road.

"Some fish for you, Mrs. Walmsley," he'd said to the pleasant faced young woman that answered his knock. "Sorry I'm late, but I fell asleep."

Her smile couldn't have been warmer, or more inviting, if he'd presented her with the crown jewels.

"Thank you" she'd replied, "but don't call me Mrs., it makes me feel old. My name's Betty." Then, taking the fish, and eyeing the boy speculatively, "If you're not going anywhere special, why not come in for a few minutes and have a drink? You can tell me how Dad's been treating you, and all about the trip." Without waiting for a reply, she led the way into the tiny, but comfortable, front room.

"Sit here," she said, patting the seat of the sofa positioned in front of the fire, "I'll put this fish away, then I'll get you a drink."

Two minutes later she returned, drew the heavy blackout curtains, switched on the standard lamp in the corner, moved across to the sideboard on the other side of the room and poured out two measures of Kings Liqueur, an over generous one for him, but hardly damping her own glass. Setting the drinks on the coffee table, she planted herself on the sofa close beside him, her hand resting lightly on his knee.

"There you are," she purred, "Get that down you and tell me about the trip."

The unfamiliar taste of neat whiskey burnt the inside of his mouth. He would have preferred Vimto but decided this wasn't the time to broadcast his immaturity; all trawlermen drank whiskey, didn't they.

As he expressed his hero-worship of 'Old Grievsie', and recounted the hardships of the voyage, he felt the spirit he had gulped warming his inside, became uneasily aware of her warmth and nearness, and the smell of her gained ascendancy over the whiskey fumes. Fascinated, his eyes moved from her face, and limpid brown eyes, in which, had he been more experienced, he would have read the brazen invitation, to the dark valley between her half-exposed breasts, visible between the parted front of the now unbuttoned blouse she was wearing.

"You poor dear," she whispered, and transferring her hand from his knee to round his shoulder, pulled him closer till their bodies touched, and kissed him on the mouth, lightly at first, then as she felt him respond, more fiercely, her tongue darting in and out of his mouth, her fingers digging into the muscles of his shoulder.

As the excitement in him built up, he felt her unbutton his flies and take out his rock hard penis. From somewhere she had produced a Durex, and as gentle fingers started to fit it over his erect member his excitement came to a climax, and his semen spurted over her hand and down the front of her skirt.

If she was disappointed it didn't show.

"You are in a hurry, Pet," she cooed, as, first doing a mopping up operation with a nappy, she put a record on the gramophone. "I like Vera Lynn, don't you, John," she said, settling on the sofa again, and starting to nibble his ear.

The second time it had been better. He had lost his virginity on the rug in front of the fire, to the accompaniment of Vera Lynn singing something about bluebirds, and the periodic rumble of the trams that rattled along the track a few yards from the window.

It was after midnight when she had led him down the backyard, and showed him out of the rear gate. "When you come round next trip come the back way, sweet," she advised. "I'll leave it unbolted if its safe."

He'd been round to see Betty every trip since that first visit, and each time she'd taught him something new in the loving game, always in front of the fire in the front room. He'd never been upstairs. Once, when they had an extra day in dock, he had suggested they went to bed but she'd demurred.

"No, John," she'd said, "it doesn't seem right with Harry so far away."

He had accepted her argument though he didn't follow the logic of it. A screw was a screw whether you had it on the rug or in a bed he thought.

When the deckies were boasting about their amorous exploits he would have loved to have expounded every detail of his affair with Betty, but for the life of him, he daren't. He liked this ship, but if the Old Man ever got to know that he was screwing his darling daughter he would skin him alive. He shuddered at the thought. Perhaps it would be best if he didn't go round again, but deep down he knew he would. The bait was too tempting to resist.

The clang of the wheelhouse door slamming broke in on his thoughts and he glanced up to see the skipper, elbows on the veranda rail, staring though the glasses into the fog ahead. He stood up and leaned over the bulwarks to see round the legs of the after gallows that blocked his view forward, and tried to focus his gaze in the direction the Skipper's binoculars were pointing.

At first he saw nothing but the swirling mist that seemed to form an impenatratable barrier. Craning his neck to see round the gallows he glanced up in the direction of the wheelhouse. The Old Man was still there; still peering forward. He transferred his gaze back to the fog ahead.

Then he saw it. First, an indistinct dark patch

against the background of grey, which as he stared, seemed to solidify into a tangible shape low on the surface of the water. As the shape drew nearer it assumed an identity. He could distinguish the lines of a small boat, and the outline of the sole occupant sitting in the stern. Closer still, discernible detail increased with nearness. He saw that the boat was ship's lifeboat, the remnant of varnish around the bow blistered and scorched, the outboard sides of the planking black and charred, evidence that at some time in the past it had been exposed to the intense heat of an inferno. The green ribbon of scum and marine growth along its waterline a certain indication that it had been in the water a long time.

It was only when the boat came amidships, almost near enough to touch with a boat hook, that the gruesome horror of what he was seeing registered, his senses recording messages his brain desperately wanted to reject. His stomach muscles knotted, he hardly noticed the bitter taste of bile rise up in his throat, and his half-digested breakfast spewed out over the half basket of cleaned prawns.

How long ago the thing sitting in the stern of the boat had relinquished its grip on life God only knows. Had it once had companions who, when the food and water had ran out, had died of hunger, dehydration, or exposure, until only it was left? Or had it been alone the whole time, scanning the horizon of some far away ocean, searching in vain for the rescuer that never came, till death released it from solitude and insanity.

Now, it sat upright in the stern of the boat, the fleshless fingers of one hand locked round the tiller, the other hand resting on the gunwale; the tattered remains of a shirt barely covering bones bleached white by a tropical sun; heart, liver, and other meaty parts long since gone, probably having provided a hors-d'oeuvre for gluttonous seabirds to fight over. Empty eye sockets stared at them accusingly, and as the boat bobbed on the gentle swell the skull seemed to throw them a hideous grin as it nodded up and down as if in greeting.

With the eyes of man and boy fixed on it, the boat drifted astern, the head seemingly nodding farewell, sightless eyes fixed on some distant horizon only it could see, it continued its eternal journey; a silent, obscene monument of man's inhumanity to man. As it passed astern the trawler's wash caused the head to bob more violently, as if screaming at them that they'd come too late, then the swirling mist closed in like a curtain, hiding the horror from them.

As the boat and its gruesome pilot disappeared into the fog, Charles Hargrieves felt a surge of sympathy. Not for the thing in the boat; that was long past any assistance he could render, and he'd experienced death too often in too many forms to be unduly affected emotionally by what he had just witnessed. No, his sympathy reached out to the young lad on the deck, now resting his head on the rail and sobbing uncontrollably.

"The poor kid's going to see worse things than that before this bloody war's over," he thought, then "I must be going soft in my old age" and checking the clock "time we had a look at the gear." and rang the engine room telegraph to signal hauling time.

Author's Note:

There was a trawler called Springwell fishing from Fleetwood during the war, but I never sailed in her, and she wasn't the ship in the story. Skipper Charlie Hargrieves and his background are products of my imagination. They are not real but they could have been.

The girl in the story was very real, but her name wasn't Betty, and although she lived within earshot of the Blackpool - Fleetwood tramway, her house wasn't in Radcliffe Road. It all happened a long time ago, and I wonder if she will remember. If she is still alive and reads this, I am sure she will recognize the lengths to which I have gone to preserve her anonymity. I have no wish to join the Kiss and Tell Brigade at my time of life.

Mending the net.

The Hull trawler 'Imperialist'.

Chapter Five

ICELAND

The Iceland the trawlermen get to know, and learn to detest, is far removed from the Iceland depicted in the glossy brochures handed out by the Tourist Board, airlines, and package holiday companies. Few, if any, of the fishermen can boast acquaintance with the hot water springs that power the central heating systems in Reykjavik, the country's capital, and the almost tropical vegetation that sprouts around those springs might just as well be on the moon as far as they are concerned.

The island has an area of about 40,000 square miles, and a population of 200,000 hardy souls whose living is almost entirely derived from the fisheries. In common with most fishermen, my knowledge of the interior is sketchy, and is confined to the thousand miles of rugged coast line, the desolate bays and fiords that cut into the mainland and provide a haven from the frequent storms that plague the region; the small fishing villages, usually situated at the head of the fiord, where stores and the services of an engineering workshop can be obtained at a price, and the numerous volcanic isles, rocks and reefs that lie off-shore always ready to rip the bottom out of an unwary boat.

Close inshore the scenery is grand. Craggy, sheer cliffs set against a background of snow-capped peaks, whose beauty is probably only rivalled by that of the northern Norwegian terrain.

When seen on a fine summer afternoon it is difficult to appreciate the barren, hostile, blizzard-swept region it becomes in the winter. It is in this later guise that Iceland presents itself to the trawlermen as they run for shelter in the fiords. Then the tops of the cliffs lining the fiord are shrouded in thick, low cloud, and above the tops of the breakers pounding the shoreline the landscape is snow white, like the pictures on Christmas cards; that is when it is visible through the curtain of driving snow and spray. More often than not, the only indication of the nearness of land is the blips on the radar screen, or the sound of the breakers pounding the feet of the cliffs. Before the introduction of radar, although the fiords provided shelter from the storm, entering them was always a risky business that required careful navigation, and considerable local knowledge, if the trawler was not to end up a statistic. I have sailed round Iceland many times over the years, and if there are any trees on the island, I've never seen one.

I made my first trip to Iceland in the spring of 1944 in the Unita. Built in 1913 by Cook, Welton, and Gemmel at Beverley, 130 feet long, 23 feet beam, and 296 tons gross, she was typical of the ships that voyaged to Iceland in the spring and summer during the war years. Very few trawlers fished at Iceland in winter at that time. Allied merchant ships suffered horrendous losses in the North Atlantic, but it wasn't fear of the U-Boat packs that deterred the fishermen. Almost all the trawlers had been taken over by the Admiralty at the start of hostilities, and those that remained fishing were either too small, or too long in the tooth to survive the Icelandic winters.

In voyaging to Iceland these ships were operating outside the range they were designed for, and as a consequence they had problems carrying sufficient bunkers. All of them were coal burners, and had bunker capacity to stay at sea for about fifteen days if steaming time was limited to three or four days. Steaming at full speed, a trawler will burn nearly twice as much coal as when she is fishing, and as the return trip to Iceland involves at least eight days steaming, ways had to be devised to carry the extra coal required. Most of the boats solved this problem by carrying a couple of days steaming coal in sacks stowed on the foredeck. Two days out of port they would drop anchor in Broad Bay, on the east side of Lewis, and empty the bags into the wings of the bunkers, thus replacing the coal that had been burnt, and clearing the deck for the often stormy passage across the exposed ocean between the Shetland Islands and the south coast of Iceland. Often, these ships would leave the Icelandic fishing grounds with just sufficient coal to get them to Stornaway where they would load the bunkers required to complete the passage to Fleetwood.

Stornaway, capital of the Western Isles and now a thriving tourist centre, was a pleasant oasis for the trawlermen. Most of the locals came from fishing stock, and we were always made welcome. The bars that fronted the harbour served good ale and the local malt. Woollen sea jerseys knitted by the crofters, which repelled seawater and never seemed to wear out, could be bought at a very reasonable price from the Fishermens Mission, and a suit length of Harris tweed could be obtained for a fraction of the price charged on the mainland high streets.

Coaling at Stornaway was done at an old wooden hulk anchored in the harbour. A gang of brawny Islanders, stripped to the waist, slaved in the bowels of the hulk, shovelling the coal into a large bucket. The coal was then heaved up, about a ton at a time, and tipped on to the deck of the trawler, and down the open bunker lids. Some years after the end of the war the Portugal, as the hulk was called, came to a sad end. The story comes from Sandy Morrice, a well-respected Aberdeen long liner skipper.

All wooden hulls leak to some extent, and according to Sandy, Mr. Duncan MacIver, who owned the coal hulk, caulked her leaking seams with a mixture of horse manure and straw. Early morning on the 17th January 1951 the Fleetwood trawler Urka collided with the midships section of the Portugal, sinking her. When Mr. Macdonald, MacIver's foreman, reported for work that morning, only her mast was visible above the water. Reporting the incident to his employer, the foreman is reputed to have commented, "It will take more than hoss shit to keep the Portugal afloat today, Sir."

The Unita, like a few of the trawlers, was built with a tunnel that connected the stokehold to the fish room. In these ships the extra coal required for the steam to Iceland was stowed in the after end of the fish room and shovelled through the tunnel at the same rate that it was being burnt. The general practice was to carry just enough coal in the fish hold to get the trawler to the fishing grounds, so that on arrival the heavy tunnel door could be fixed in place, and the hold washed out and made ready for the expected catch.

The Unita carried a crew of sixteen men: Skipper, mate, bosun, five deckhands, two decky-trimmers, two engineers, two firemen, a cook, and a 'brassie'. I was signed on as decky-trimmer. On the passage to Iceland the trimmers worked watch on, watch off, with the engineers, moving the coal from the fish room, through the tunnel into the stokehold for the firemen to burn; about ten tons per day. For the first couple of watches the going was easy, the work becoming progressively harder. When the ship left the dock the tunnel would be full, so the coal didn't have to be moved far. Once the tunnel was emptied you cleared all the middle part of the hold, then began to work on the pounds farthest from the tunnel door. The easiest way to move the coal was to fill a basket, and drag it, four or five stone at a time, through the tunnel to the stokehold. This was hard graft, not made any easier by the fact that the tunnel was only about four feet high, and you had the roll of the ship to contend with.

Once the fish room was empty of coal, or the trawler arrived on the fishing grounds, the decky-trimmers vacated the stokehold and took on a deckhand's normal duties. For the extra four days toil moving the coal the trimmers were paid one pound, an amount which scarcely paid for the gear

that was ruined.

I spent the spring and summer of 1944 and 1945 fishing at Iceland. Having listened so many times to the old hands recounting tales about the hardship and peril to be endured on these grounds, I was more than a little excited and apprehensive at the prospect, but in the event the reality was an anticlimax. Weatherwise, if you discount the long passage to and from the fishing grounds, the fishing was little different to working round the Orkney and Shetland Isles. Not a trace of the black frost I had heard so much about.

The biggest difference between fishing in home waters and fishing at Iceland was in the size of the catches. The huge hauls of fish, consisting mainly of cod, were heaved in over the starboard side, and as soon as the trawl was shot we started gutting. There was no watch below. Gutting what fish we could between hauls, the fishing continued until the deck was filled to capacity. Then we pulled the net inboard, and laid while we cleared the fish off the deck. When the deck was nearly clear, over the side went the trawl, and the whole process started again. Sometimes, during periods of heavy fishing, we would be working sixty or seventy hours without a break. When eventually the Old Man did decide to give us a three or four hour nap we would crawl into our bunks, still wearing our deck gear, and completely knackered. It seemed we'd only just closed our eyes when we would be called out, our bodies still crying out for sleep, to start work again. Until the fish hold was full the toil would continue. Only when a gale of wind suspended fishing operations could we expect to get a proper sleep.

The Icelandic Cod Wars were still some time in the future, and the fishing limits were set at three miles. It may surprise the reader to learn that even when the trawlers were allowed to fish as close to the land as three miles a considerable amount of poaching took place. I suppose it is a fact of life that whenever a fence is erected, the grass on the wrong side of the fence will always appear to be greener.

The only other significant difference that I could see at that time between home water and distant water fishing was that in the distant water boats we received a ration of duty free cigarettes, tobacco, and rum.

Throughout the war, and the first couple of years after, fish was sold at a maximum controlled price at the port fish markets, and as a result, aboard the trawlers the accent was on quantity rather than quality. Providing the Port Health Officer passed the fish as fit for human consumption, rubbish was sold for the same price as prime fish, hence the more fish you could cram down the hold, the more money you earned. This state of affairs continued until controls were removed in 1949.

By 1946 the Admiralty was returning the trawlers for fishing, and that year I sampled the delights of an Icelandic winter. The Red Knight was the ship, owned by Iago Steam Fishing Company, and commanded by Skipper Eric Littler. We spent part of the winter fishing for hake at St. Kilda, and the remainder catching plaice and pneumonia off the north west coast of Iceland. That year the winter was relatively mild, but I received a foretaste of what was to come. The following summer, in the same ship, I made my first trip to Bear Island. We

came home with a full hold, 2,450 ten-stone kits of codling, which sold for £4,500. That was the last time I sailed from Fleetwood.

Chapter Six

GRIMSBY AND THE NORTHERN BOATS

By this time my father had been demobilized and had returned to fishing. Besides releasing the men, the Admiralty was also returning the big distant water trawlers. H. Markham Cook, the company my father worked for, had moved back to Grimsby at the end of the war, and in the summer of 1947 my family moved to fish from that port.

The next three or four years were boom times as far as distant water trawling was concerned, and the trawler owners made millions. The fishing grounds around Bear Island, Spitzbergen, and the Barents Sea had not been fished for five years, and fish stocks had multiplied. These waters teemed with fish, and there was a ready market for it in the United Kingdom.

The Northern Boats, owned by Markham Cook, were the ideal ships to exploit the conditions. Built at Bremerhaven in 1936, and over 188 feet long, they were the biggest, most powerful trawlers afloat at that time. Besides being the fastest ships working from the Humber ports, they also had the biggest fishrooms, so in a period of dip and fill it was not hard to earn money in them.

Here the accent is on the word *EARN*. From the trawlerman's point of view they were floating work-houses.

I spent the best part of the next twenty years aboard the Northern Boats, my first ship sailing from Grimsby being the Northern Dawn, commanded by Skipper Bob Blyth.

Then they had a complement of twenty-eight men, which included eighteen deckhands. Six of the deckies lived in the fo'c'sle for'ard, the remaining twelve being housed in a large cabin that formed the bottom level of the three-tier bridge superstructure. The level above this cabin held the skipper's accommodation and the wireless room, while the top storey comprised the wheelhouse and chartroom. The mate, bosun, engineers, firemen and cook were berthed aft, and the wireless operator had a bunk in the wireless room. All hands took their meals in a large messroom situated aft side of the galley at deck level.

Originally, fifteen Northern Class ships were built. Three of them, *Northern Isles*, *Northern Princess*, and *Northern Rover* were lost while on Admiralty service during the war. Three more, the *Northern Chief*, *Northern Gift* and *Northern Reward* were sold to Icelandic owners early in 1947. The remaining nine, *Northern Dawn*, *Duke*, *Foam*, *Gem*, *Pride*, *Sun*, *Sky*, *Spray* and *Wave* worked from Grimsby. Except for *Northern Spray*, which was wrecked at Iceland in 1964 and declared a total loss, they all ended at the breakers yard between 1964 and 1966.

German shipbuilders knew trawling, and put a lot of thought into the design of these ships. The end product was a highly efficient fish catching tool. Their huge triple expansion engines were fitted with an exhaust steam turbine that generated 1,000 I.H.P. and made for a turn of speed no other trawler could match. Even with a block in the expansion in the interest of fuel economy, we could make between 13 and 14 knots in reasonable weather. On one occasion, when running in with an injured man, with the block removed and using wet steam, the Northern Gem made the passage from Bear Island to Honingsvaag at an average speed of 16 knots, and while on Admiralty service the Northern Spray was reputed to have reached a speed of 17 knots while chasing and ramming a U-Boat.

Initially the Northern Boats were coal burners, and the after fishroom could be blanked off and used to carry coal for the long steam to the fishing grounds. What made them different to the British built ships was that the tunnel connecting fishroom and stokehold had sufficient headroom to allow the trimmers to stand upright, and was fitted with rails on which a truck ran, thus eliminating the need to drag the coal aft in baskets.

On passage to the fishing grounds, we worked three bridge watches with three men in each watch. The mate and bosun each took charge of a watch, and there were three deckies in the third watch. Most of the older hands had recently been demobilized, and had got their mates or skippers tickets while in the service, so it was never difficult to find a certificated man to take charge of the deckies

watch. In the Grimsby ships you were never paid for taking on this responsibility, although I believe that in the Hull boats the man in charge of the third watch was dubbed Fourth Hand, and paid an extra six-pence a day for his trouble. So much for the belief that we were well paid for our labour. I took my mate's ticket in 1949, and before that date, I can recall trips in the Northern Gem when I was the only man on deck that couldn't boast holding a mate's or skipper's ticket. That gives some idea of the competition to gain and retain a command in one of the big trawlers.

Three of the remaining eleven deckies would work with the firemen trimming the coal out of the fishroom, while the rest were employed as daymen.

Another feature unique to the Northern Boats was the size of the net store. It was at least twice as big as on any other trawler I had sailed in. With net bins either side, the middle working space was big enough to allow a full trawl to be stretched out and rigged, and there was still room for the bosun to rig his codends. The fo'c'sle, where the daymen lived, was situated over the net store, and there was a bunker lid that gave access from fo'c'sle to net store so that in bad weather work could continue down the hold without having to unbatten the hatches.

Soon after being released from the navy, the ships were converted, one or two at a time, to burn oil instead of coal, and this made them even better working ships, but increases in the price of oil halted the conversion programme, and Northern Dawn and Northern Pride remained coal burners all their working lives.

On arrival at the fishing grounds, the deck crew was divided into four watches, five men in a watch. You worked three six-hour watches on deck, and had one watch off, 'eighteen and six' as it was called. But to say that the men had six hours below after doing their eighteen-hour spell on deck would be telling a lie.

'Eighteen and five' would be a more truthful description of the work to sleep ratio. The watches were changed at 0030 hours, 0630 hours, 1230 hours and 1830 hours, while the meals, served in two thirty-minute sittings, were dished up at 0600, 1200, and 1800. The watch turning out had to take their meal first sitting, thus losing thirty minutes of their watch below, and the watch going below took their meal second sitting, again losing half an hour.

All these meals were substantial affairs, and were a necessity if you were to maintain the energy required to complete the gruelling work cycle over a period of 10 days or more. No engine will run without fuel, and a little thought will show that you lost half an hour for refuelling at each end of your watch, thus reducing sleeping time to five hours.

Refuelling is the only word I can think of that adequately describes the meals while the trawler was fishing. Although the food was good and wholesome, often dished up in a way that was a tribute to the culinary arts, there were none of the pleasures usually associated with a good meal. Going off the deck at the end of our eighteen-hour stint, hungry and exhausted, we would cram down as much food as our stomachs would hold as quickly as we could, then drag ourselve off to our bunks. Five hours later, one of the watch going below would enter the fo'c'sle bellowing "WATCH-O" and rudely shake us awake. Still half asleep, we would crawl out of the cosy heat of our bunks, pull on the few items of clothing we had stripped off before turning in, and maybe have a few puffs on a cigarette. By the time we were able to coax overtired leg muscles to carry us aft to the messroom we would have ten or fifteen minutes left to stuff down as much fuel as our tanks would hold without rejecting it before it was time to relieve the watch on deck going below. We didn't talk much for the first couple of hours on deck. Still suffering from the shock of the rude awakening before our blood cells had been sufficiently recharged, stomach juices working overtime to digest the sudden intake of food, and the knowledge that another eighteen hours backbreaking toil separated us from our bunks were hardly factors likely to instigate polite conversation.

Eighteen hours continuous heavy physical work a day, in any conditions, is far too heavy a burden to expect any man to endure over an extended period. Trawling was highly dangerous work, and Government statistics show that more men were killed and maimed aboard the trawlers than in any other industry. A large proportion of these accidents were due to men working in conditions that would make any self respecting union man throw up his hands in horror, with their reflexes dulled by lack of adequate sleep.

Until the early fifties, with the sole exception of Northern Wave, commanded by the Icelandic skipper August Ebernezersson, although spending winter and summer on the Arctic fishing grounds, the Northern Boats rarely visited Iceland. Bear Island and the

Barents Sea were their main hunting grounds.

The annual work cycle, beginning in early January, would start with fishing the grounds along the Norwegian coast. Starting at Skraven, we would follow the fish north to Andenes, Swinsgrun, and Malangen Bank, finishing the Coast Season at the end of March on North West Bank. The prey would be the large shoals of big cod, full of roe, that spawned along the edge of the continental shelf in the deep water between 150 and 250 fathoms. The best cod fishing occurred in the daylight, and as a rule, we caught enough cod to keep the crew gutting all night. On those days when we were unlucky enough to miss out on the daytime fishing, there were good bags of coley and haddock to be had in the shoal water on top of the banks during the night.

A feature peculiar to trawling along this part of the Norwegian coast was that the ships only towed the trawl in one direction, to the northeast. The strong tides, and the steepness of the edge made this a necessity. The cod tended to keep to narrow limits as regards the depth of water they spawned in. The edge of the shelf was so steep, sheer as the side of a house in places, that the distance of a ship's length at right angles to the direction of the run of the edge resulted in a difference in the depth of water of 100 fathoms or more. Consequently, all the ships wanted their gear down along a very narrow band, and to have attempted to tow in both directions would have resulted in either fouling the gear of the ships towing the other way, or taking evading action that caused your gear to be off the bottom for most of the tow. In practice, we shot our

gear to the northeast, and held the depth of water we wanted to be in till hauling time. After hauling we steamed back to the starting point and repeated the process. At times there have been half a dozen ships queueing up to shoot.

From April to August we worked the waters around Bear Island and Spitzbergen. These waters teemed with fish, for the most part half grown codling. Picking out the biggest fish for gutting, 80 per cent or more of the catch would be booted back through the scuppers, to be gobbled up by the screaming seagulls that hovered round the ship. All round the clock the carnage would continue. It was like the slaughter of the innocents. I can recall trips at Bear Island when, for the last twenty-four hours work, we have spent the time between hauls just sorting out the big fish, and washing the small fry back overboard. When we finally left for home the decks would be plastered with fish as high as the tops of the bulwarks, from the breakwater on the whaleback to the trawl winch, and down the port side as far as the galley. Sometimes we would still be gutting when we passed Skonvar Light, the southern-most tip of the Lotofen Islands, over 400 miles south of Bear Island. On average we landed about 4,500 ten stone kits of headless fish each three week trip, and in the process of catching it must have killed ten times that amount of codling. I don't know how long it takes a codling to reach maturity, but our wholesale plundering can have done little to help the conservation of future fish stocks.

As far as fishing was concerned, September was a slack month. The month the regular skippers took their holidays, and those mates with skipper's tickets took the ships away. If you were lucky there might be good hauls of cod outside the 100 fathom line southeast of Seahorse Island (Hope Island on Admiralty charts), or on the Green Mud Banks to the northeast, but the fishing was always patchy. You either hit the jackpot or you caught nothing at all. What the trawlermen described as "Catch me - Fuck me" fishing.

From the beginning of October until the start of the Coast Season in January we worked the Barents Sea grounds around Skolpen Bank, the North Deeps, and as far east as the west coast of Novaya Zemlya. Away from the warming influence of the northern extremities of the Gulf Stream, this was the time of the year you needed your winter woollies with you. If you check the temperature inside a commercial freezer you'll probably find it is somewhere between -20 and -30 degrees Centigrade. We frequently had to work on deck in temperatures of -50 or -60 degrees. We must have been idiots.

During these winter months, all the ships working in the Barents Sea took advantage of the shelter afforded by the Norwegian fiords to ease part of their passage. After a 12 hour steam up West Fiord, keeping under the lee of the Lotofen Islands, we would pick up a pilot at Lodigen for the twenty-four hour journey through the northern fiords. Completely landlocked, these ribbons of water wind their way through the myriad islands and reefs that abound off the Norwegian Arctic coast, in places so narrow that there is only room for one way traffic.

Although sheltered from the wind, before the introduction of reliable radar equipment, in a confined space the frequent heavy snow falls that re-

duced visibility to zero were an ever present danger to navigation. Before entering the fiords we would rig up a snow anchor. Heaving up the port anchor cable from the chain locker, we would break the cable at the second shackle, and shackle the anchor end of the cable to the trawl warp. Then we would heave the slack cable on to the trawl winch. Now, if snow made it necessary, we could anchor in minutes in water as deep as 700 fathoms, until the snowfall ceased and visibility was restored.

Throughout the winters of 1947 and 1948, when the Northern Boats disembarked the pilots at Honingsvaag, at the northern end of the fiords, they would take on five or six Norwegian fishermen to complement their twenty-eight men crews. This gives some indication of the size of the fish shoals waiting to be harvested.

While the above account gives a fairly general idea of the trawler fleet's movements throughout the year, it should not be regarded as on a par with the ten commandments. The trawlermen were hunters, and fish were where you found them. The skipper used his experience to decide where the trawler fished, and I never sailed with one that didn't have his own ideas.

One group of men who bucked the general trend fished for plaice at the eastern end of the Barents Sea. The plaice season lasted for about six weeks, from mid-November till Christmas, and was cold work, with another trip to be had about Easter-time. The control price of flatfish was considerably higher than that of round fish, which explains why it was the smaller class of ship, whose smaller fishroom placed them at a disadvantage when bulk fishing, that exploited the plaice fishery. Skipper Tess Johnston was the acknowledged expert on these grounds, and after retiring from the sea, worked for the White Fish Authority producing fishing charts for the area. W.F.A. could not have recruited a better man.

The main area the plaice is caught lies just to the north of the entrance to the White Sea, and along the west side of the gully that runs off from Cape Cherni. To understand why the plaice migrates to this area when it does you need to know something about the climate and oceanography of the region. One arm of the Gulf Stream flows round North Cape, Norway, and turning eastward, continues along the Norwegian and Russian Arctic coasts. Relatively warm, it keeps these coastal waters free of ice. At some point east of Cape Kanin the Gulf Stream meets the cold water stream which flows westward from the Kara Sea through the gap between the southern tip of Novaya Zemlya and the coast of Siberia. On meeting, both streams turn north and flow, parallel with each other, along the west coast of Novaya Zemlya. The White Sea is a shallow, landlocked expanse of water, no more than thirty fathoms deep, and is entered though the forty mile wide passage between Svetinos and Cape Kanin. In November the intensely cold winds, blowing from the desolate wastes of Siberia, cause the shoal water in the White Sea to freeze over. The main port, Archangel, can only be kept open by the continuous use of an ice-breaker. As the sea freezes, the plaice are forced to flee in search of warmer water. Trawling in the White Sea is prohibited, but as the ice forces the fish to evacuate their summer feeding grounds they are concentrated in a small area just outside, and to the west, of the entrance, and are easy prey for the trawlers waiting to scoop them up. In late spring the reverse process occurs. As the water temperature in the White Sea rises the plaice flock back to their feeding grounds and are once again concentrated in a small area. The secret to success is knowing where to be, and when to be there.

Over the years I've landed a few good trips of flats from the White Sea, but whenever I think of plaice fishing one particular trip in the winter of 1948 springs to mind.

I was decky with Bill Woods in the Northern Duke at the time, and we shot the gear among a small group of ships working very close to the land between the Verona Rocks and the Russian naval base on Kildin Island. We had two one-hour tows, and each time the net came up full of plaice; all big fish, three and four pounders almost as big as dustbin lids. While hauling the gear the second time a Russian gunboat came charging off towards the trawlers, firing starshells as it approached, so Woody decided that discretion was the better part of valour, and we pulled the gear aboard and left the area. We put over 500 kits of plaice down the fishroom for the two hauls. One of the ships in the group, the Kirknes, owned by Littles and commanded by Skipper Keli Sigurssen, managed to complete a full trip on this ground and landed a bumper trip; over 3,800 kit, nearly all plaice which grossed over £18,000. These figures constituted Grimsby port records, both for grossing, and for the weight of plaice landed in one trip. The latter record still stands and is never likely to be beaten.

But trawling can be a cruel game in more ways than one. One of the Butt Group's smaller ships, found the above fish shop, and left for home with over 2,000 kits of plaice on board, a marvellous trip for the class of ship. Approaching the northern end of the fiords, and having a bit of spare time for the market he was going for, the skipper decided to have one more haul, and was arrested by a Norwegian gunboat. Found guilty of trawling inside Norwegian fishing limits, his catch and gear was confiscated. My sympathies were not with the skipper, they were with the men on deck, who, due to an act of stupidity, were robbed of the pay for all the toil they had put in.

Another very successful Arctic fisherman who never followed the herd was Skipper Norman Rogers, the unofficial Prince of Poachers. Norman worked the inshore grounds along Norway's Arctic coast all the year round, and probably knew more about this region than any man alive. I've heard tell that in the years of depression before the war he carried an out-of-work Norwegian pilot with him all the time he was on the fishing grounds, which would account for his encyclopedic knowledge of the area. I sailed under him in the Prince Philip, and working for him was an education. During the time I spent with him we never trawled during the daylight hours, and I can't recall ever fishing for two consecutive nights in the same place. Every trip the work pattern was similar. We would shoot the gear about tea time, work though the night till breakfast time, then pull the gear aboard and change the scenery. As often as not we would spend part of the day time tied up to the quay in one of the small fishing harbours (Harstad, Tromso, Hammerfest, Honingsvaag or Vardo), and leaving at teatime, we would have the gear down within an hour or two. Norman had a host of friends and contacts ashore, and to get away with the amount of illegal fishing we indulged in, must have had reliable information regarding the movements of the fishery protection ships. The Norwegian government paid a reward to any of the coastal steamers that reported trawlers fishing in prohibited areas, but if we were ever reported, spending only one night in the same place, we were always gone before the gunboat arrived. Sometimes, working without deck and navigation lights, we would be towing the gear so close to the land we could hear the breakers pounding the shore. In the intense darkness of the Arctic night, I've mended the net by the light of a hand-held electric torch, and shooting the gear, we had to have a man hold a stick on the warps as they ran out, calling out when the marks caused the stick to jump.

Supremely confident in his own ability, and completely devoid of nerves, I'd rate Norman Rogers as the finest seaman, and the most experienced trawlerman I ever floated with. While unable to do much about the temperature in those frozen regions, he could control the wind, or at least, control the effects of the wind. No matter how hard it blew, or whichever direction it blew from, Norman was always able to get into some cove or fiord where we could work in the shelter of a lee shore. We often worked in freezing conditions, but never with water up to our waist. I learnt more about the Norwegian coast while sailing under Norman than in all the other years I spent at sea.

The following episode demonstrates the man's confidence and his knowledge of the region. The passage through the northern fiords from Lodigen to Honingsvaag involves the navigation of over 250 miles of narrow channels that wind their way through islets, rocks, and reefs, with frequent heavy snowfalls reducing visibility to zero. Norwegian law dictates that all vessels proceeding through these fiords must carry a Government licensed pilot, a dictate supported, in the case of British trawlers, by a directive from the U.K. mutual insurance clubs. In the years immediately after the war we carried one pilot, but a strike by the pilots, who successfully argued that the passage was too long for one man, resulted in two pilots being carried.

We hove to just off the entrance to Lodigen harbour to embark the pilots, and as soon as they had climbed over the bulwarks and the pilot boat had moved off, Norman rang the Prince Philip's engines full ahead, and we moved up the fiord. It was usual practice for the pilots to be offered the skipper's cabin for the trip, no other accommodation being available, but the Prince Philip had a small cabin abaft the wheelhouse for their use. On being shown to the pilot's cabin, and no doubt wanting the extra comfort the master's accommodation offered, these two young men came to the wheelhouse, complained about the accommodation they had been offered, and refused to take the ship through the fiords unless they were better housed.

Rogers eyed the two young men with some amusement.

"I'm sorry I've nowhere else to put you, gentle-men," he said, "and I certainly can't afford to waste time taking you back to Lodigen, so you'll just have to come along for the ride. I'll put you both ashore at Honingsvaag."

The two pilots retreated from the wheelhouse, confident that before we reached the narrows at Rifness the skipper would cave in to their demands. They didn't know the calibre of the man they were dealing with. Taking the tricky stretches himself, and with the mate, Jimmy Cormack, and I sharing the more straight forward bits, we completed the passage without allowing our striking pilots on the bridge. On arrival at Honingsvaag, without their papers being signed, two very subdued young men disembarked on to the pilot boat. Their tactics might have worked with any skipper other than Norman Rogers.

Norman also had the reputation of being a hard man, but I found that his bark was much worse than his bite. He was the only Grimsby distant water skipper I ever sailed with that didn't work a watch below, but as we were only fishing half the day most of the time, this was of little consequence. We got a fair share of sleep. Although he must have been nearing sixty years of age when I sailed with him, whenever we were working on the deck on the outward passage, or putting a new set of gear alongside when on the fishing ground, you would always find him on deck, pulling his guts out with the rest of the lads. Do your whack of the graft and you were O.K., but try to hang the latch and he'd go through you like a dose of salts. Hard as nails himself, he had short shrift for anyone foolish enough to complain of a minor ailment. One of my watchmates, an Aberdeen lad, came up to the bridge making quite a fuss about a big salt water boil on his arm, a common affliction that plagued the fishermen. Norman examined the boil, and the remedy he advocated was typical of the man, and not very sympathetic.

"Go down and get a new gutting knife," he said, keeping a straight face, "John will hold your arm down, and I'll slice the top off, pour a drop of iodine in the hole, and stick a plaster over it. You'll be as right as rain in the morning."

The recipient of this cold blooded advice left the bridge, and didn't return until the skipper had turned in, but needless to say, it was the last we heard about Deenie's boil. A trip or two later Norman was suffering, and in considerable pain, from a carbuncle on his neck. My comment that I had a new, sharp gutting knife in my drawer produced a wry grin, and the loss of his company for the rest of the watch.

Over the years, Norman had gathered together a crew as hard as he was, as good a bunch of shipmates as you'd find anywhere. Jimmy, the mate, was a dour scot, an expert at his job, tough as leather, and as good as two men when there was graft to be done. Other members of the deck crew readily spring to mind. Frank, a Grimsby man, was a glutton for work and girlie magazines. Arthur, strong as two horses, and Reg, an artist on the trawl and with a marine spike, were two of the deckies, a couple of Fleetwood lads who had learned their trade in the same hard school I was brought up in, sailing from the Lancashire fishing port.

In the evenings, on passage to and from the fishing grounds, we used to play a pretty rough, boisterous game we called King of the Castle. One of the lads, the King, would climb on the messdeck table. The object of the game was to knock or drag the King off the table. Whoever succeeded in accomplishing this became King and took his place on the table top. Often the ship would be bouncing about in heavy seas, so it's a wonder no one ever broke an arm or a leg, but as I said earlier, they were a crowd of hard lads.

One trip the regular cook stopped off for a holiday, and to be charitable, his replacement wasn't the best cook in the world.

Homeward bound, we picked up the pilots at Honingsvaag, and at the same time the cook ordered a few victuals to satisfy his voracious shipmates. Among these provisions was a quantity of sausages, and these delicacies, totally unlike the British banger, came aboard in large cans. About ten inches long, and over an inch thick, they had skins like rhinoceros hide. Boiled, they appeared on the table at the first meal after leaving Honingsvaag. Pink and steaming in the platter, they looked like a pile of boiled penises, and about as appetizing. At the end of the meal they were still in the platter. They turned up on the table every meal time during the four day passage to the Humber with the same result. It seemed the cook was determined we were going to eat his sausages, the crew were equally adamant in rejecting them.

Anchored off the Lower Burcum Buoy awaiting the Grimsby Dock locks to open, I went up to the bridge to take the anchor watch. Norman was in the wheelhouse looking very stern.

"John", he said, "the cook's just been up here and complained that gang of bastards in the fo'c'sle have stretched over the galley table, pulled his pants down, and stuffed one of those sausages up his arse. Go down and give them a bollocking."

As I moved towards the door he added, "and tell 'em to stick the rest of the sausages up the same place."

If, from all the characters I met that were involved with the trawling industry, I had to nominate one man for inclusion in the New Year honours list, that man would be Norman Rogers. He would certainly make a more exciting candidate for the "This Is Your Life" series than any of the young show biz personalities that prance in front of the camera, who have never really lived, or experienced life in the raw.

Grimsby Fish Docks in days of the smacks.

Chapter Seven

GREENLAND

A small handful of intrepid skippers deviated from the regular pattern of work to voyage to the stormy, ice infested waters around Greenland, usually between June and September.

Measuring 1,670 miles long in a north-south direction, with an area of 840,000 square miles, Greenland is the largest island in the world. 85 per cent of the land is covered by a permanent ice cap that is over 10,000 feet thick in places.

Once a Danish colony, but now a part of Denmark, the island has a population of 54,000, most of whom live on the narrow coastal strip of land along the milder south west coast. Probably the first Europeans to visit Greenland were the Vikings, and the remains of old Viking settlements can be seen from seaward along the shore of Julliana Bay between Cape Farewell and Cape Desolation.

Every Arctic fishing ground presents its own particular problems and dangers to those fishermen bold enough to go there, and in this respect Greenland is no different. The first hurdle to surmount is the long steam, about 1,500 miles from the Humber to Cape Farewell, the southernmost tip of the island. No further than voyaging to the eastern part of the Barents Sea, but the difference is that 1,100 miles of the passage, from the Butt of Lewis to Farewell, is across the remote, exposed, often stormy North Atlantic, well to the north of shipping lanes, and at the western end of the trek there is the danger of encountering ice.

In the northern part of the North Atlantic the prevailing westerly wind often reaches gale force, and in mid-ocean the height of the rollers can be intimidating. One voyage in the fall of 1954 on Northern Pride, my first command, we battled against near gale force winds all the way across, averaging less than six knots, and taking over nine days to reach Cape Farewell.

It is a lonely passage. So far north of the Atlantic trade lanes the only ships you are likely to see after leaving the Butt of Lewis astern are the odd trawlers homeward bound. On arrival at Farewell the decision has to be made as to where fishing operations will commence. The grounds worked by most of the trawlers extend five or six hundred miles along the west coast, and the skipper will use any fishing reports obtained by radio from the ships already on the fishing grounds, weather forecasts, reports from the ice patrol which indicate those areas sufficiently clear of ice to allow trawling, and his own experience to make the decision.

To navigate and fish these waters you need to know something about the tidal streams and winds that govern the movement of the ice. A cold water stream flows in a circular motion from Baffin Bay along the north west coast of Greenland, turns westward across the Davis Strait somewhere south of latitude 70, and then turns north to flow along the east coast of Baffin Island. The East Greenland Current, another cold water stream, flows south along the east coast of Greenland, and keeping close in to the land as it rounds Farewell, turns north and flows along the west coast. North of Cape Desolation it turns west, crosses the Strait, and turning south forms the Labrador Current. One other current influences the fishing. In mid-Atlantic an arm of the warm, north easterly flowing Gulf Stream, the Irminger Current, flows north into the Denmark Strait, turns westward about latitude 64, and approaching the east coast of Greenland, turns south and rounds Farewell flowing outside, and parallel with the East Greenland Current. In the spring the sea ice at the edge of the polar ice cap begins to melt and break up, and the glaciers, rivers of ice hundreds of feet thick, begin to creep towards the sea. As the end of the glacier is pushed into the sea, the water gradually wears away the bottom layers of ice, forming an overhang that eventually breaks off, and an iceberg results. The glaciers of north west Greenland calve an average of 10,000 bergs a year, many of which find their way into the Atlantic. A great many of the bergs never escape. They travel south with the current, are carried west across the Davis Strait, and on reaching the coast of Baffin Island are driven northwards to be locked to the icecap when the winter frost returns to freeze the sea again.

While not so productive as the glaciers of north west Greenland, those on the east side have a greater effect on the fishing. The huge bergs they carve are carried south, and round Farewell by the East Greenland Current, and after a spell of northerly winds, are often accompanied by pack ice and tabular bergs from the melting ice cap.

Apart from the danger to navigation, these glacier bergs affect the fishing in another, less obvious way. As the glacier forces its way seaward through the valleys and ravines huge rocks and boulders become embedded in the base of the ice. As the bergs journey south they meet the warmer water of the Irminger current and the submerged part begins to melt. As melting continues the stones and boulders are released and fall to the bottom. For centuries this process has been repeated, with the result that the sea bed in the deep water round Farewell and the southern part of the Davis Strait is covered by a heap of big stones making trawling impracticable. Because of this natural phenomenon trawl fishing around Farewell is confined to the shoal water close inshore inside the fifty fathom line. The reason that the shoal water is relatively free of stones is that the big icebergs draw over eighty fathoms, so they ground before they can reach the shoals.

There are other factors besides having to work close inshore that contribute to making fishing on the Cape Farewell ground a highly dangerous business. The current which flows westerly round the Cape is very strong, and flows directly into two rocks positioned about four miles apart in an east-west direction, and about three or four miles offshore, further restricting searoom on the fishing ground. Hauling the gear in the strong tide requires extreme caution if the trawler is to be prevented from being swept on to the rocks.

Another climatic phenomenon peculiar to the area, and which affects the fishing, is the katabatic wind system. The coastline around Farewell is dominated by three very high promontories which slope steeply down to the sea. Throughout the afternoon, during the summer months, the air on the slopes heats up and rises, and as evening approaches the cold air from the high ground rushes down to fill the vacuum, creating gale-force winds and mountainous seas. This effect is purely local, and those men with experience of the locality trawl throughout the daytime, and as evening approaches steam twenty or thirty miles out to sea where they can clear the day's catch off the deck unaffected by the inshore winds.

In September 1952, the Hull trawler Norman was fishing with a small group of ships working the Cape Farewell ground. The fishing was very good, and in the late afternoon, with their decks loaded with cod, the trawlers pulled their gear aboard and steamed twenty miles or so to seaward to clear the decks. Just before dawn the next morning, in dense fog, they steamed back towards the land to resume fishing. As they approached the shoal water a Mayday call crackled over the V.H.F. radio. The Norman had grounded on the rocks and was unsure of her exact position. The fog reduced visibility to a few yards making it difficult for the other boats to locate her. Fearing the stranded vessel, her bottom probably ripped out, would slide back into deep water, her crew tried to swim to the temporary safety of the rocks, but in the icy water and strong current, they

had very little chance of survival. When the fog lifted the Norman could be seen still jammed on the rocks. Had her crew stayed on board they would probably have been rescued. In the event there was only one survivor from the complement of twenty. The galley boy, a young lad, was plucked off the rocks by a Norwegian line fishing boat. Skipper Charlie O'Neill, commanding the Hull trawler Thornella, recovered several of the bodies from the sea. Fishing the Farewell ground is certainly no job for an amateur.

The fishing along the west coast of Greenland, so far as trawling is concerned, is mainly confined to the inshore waters of Julliana bay, and the tops of the offshore banks that are relatively free of stones. In a region subjected to dense fog for most of the time, icebergs constitute the main danger, although the advent of radar alleviated much of the stress. I have seen a dozen or more bergs sailing up the Strait like a flotilla of schooners, wind and tide carrying them along faster than we were towing the gear.

Often, these ice islands ran aground on the edges of the banks, and on one trip I used a berg that had grounded in 70 fathoms (420 feet) of water on Danas Bank as a buoy for five days. It was still there when we left for home.

Trawling wasn't the only type of fishing carried out on the Greenland grounds. Norwegian and Faroese line fishermen often worked in the Davis Strait, but if any group of men led a more precarious life than the trawlermen, that distinction must go to the Portuguese dory fishermen. These hardy creatures were transported to the fishing grounds by schooner. On arrival their one-man tiny dories would be launched at first light, and the occupant would fish with a hand line all day, returning to the mother ship as darkness fell. On rejoining the schooner he would have to split and salt down his day's catch, chop bait, and prepare his lines for the next day's fishing. Only when this work was done would he get his evening meal and a sleep. At first light, with only a bottle of wine and a loaf of bread, he would be cast adrift again to endure another day's fishing in the tiny open boat. These schooners remained at sea for five months or more, and in a region where dense fog was the norm, and gale force winds sprang up with surprising rapidity, the loss of life must have been enormous. It was commonplace for the captains of the schooners to call the trawlers on the radio to inform them that a number of dories had been lost in the fog, and request that we keep a lookout for them.

A Portuguese captain once told me that it was customary among the dory fishermen for the head of the family to take on this job. If he was lost, the eldest son was expected to replace him. I can't visualize a harder way to earn a living, and it is certainly not a job I would fancy.

Regardless of where we were fishing, we only went into port when requiring essential repairs, stores, or medical assistance, so my knowledge of the Greenlanders is limited, and mostly hearsay. Generally the port officials were Danish, and the trawler crews, with the exception of the Skipper when on ship's business, were not allowed to go ashore. The reason given for this restriction was that it was imposed for health reasons; a cold or

influenza epidemic could wipe out a village.

All the benefits of the Danish social security system apply to the Greenlanders, including very generous maternity payments. Although I have no first hand experience, I have been told many times that the main ambition of the majority of the Greenland girls was to get pregnant and obtain the security afforded by the child benefit, and that when a foreign trawler was alongside the quay the combined efforts of the Danish immigration and port officials were directed at preventing the contact necessary if the girls' ambition was to become reality.

Skipper Mark (Snowy) Tomlinson commanded the Northern Spray, and spent as much time in Greenland waters as any skipper sailing from Grimsby. On one occasion the Northern Spray was the inside ship of four that were tied up to the quay in Godthaab, the capital of Greenland. The story, as I heard it, was that Snowy was aboard one of the outer ships playing solo with the other skippers. Meantime, a party of girls managed to elude the harbour security men and boarded Northern Spray. What was later described as an orgy developed. When the police eventually arrived on the quayside they found naked girls being chased up the rigging, and one young lady being given a bath in one of the liver boilers.

When Northern Spray docked at Grimsby a report of the incident had preceded her, probably via the Danish Consulate, with the result that Skipper Tomlinson was crucified by the trawler owners. The Trawler Mutual Insurance cancelled his Insurance Master's Certificate, which meant he could not command any vessel connected with that insurance company, thus terminating his fishing career. Subsequently, Snowy appealed to a civil court and won his case, but despite that court's decision, he never commanded another trawler. The man was deprived of the means of earning a living, and the episode was another example of the extent to which the trawler-owning cartel, sometimes appearing to be above the law, controlled the fish docks, and the people they employed.

The late Skipper Jim Latham was another frequent visitor to the Greenland fishing grounds, and was a big man in every sense of the word. A native of Fleetwood, and an old family friend, Jim had taken command of Northern Princess when the German builders first handed her over in 1936. When the Admiralty released the Northern Boats at the end of the war he skippered the Northern Duke, Northern Gem, and finally the Northern Princess, the first of the company's post war new buildings. The top earner in the company, probably in the port, there weren't many records he hadn't broken.

One trip at Bear Island in Northern Gem one of the deckhands, Jack Baxter, complained of stomach pains and was obviously in great distress. Jack had been with us for a long time, was a good worker, and the last man aboard that would resort to malingering.

Consequently, Jim ordered the trawl to be pulled aboard, and we set off to seek medical assistance. The nearest doctor was at Honindsvaag, over 300 miles away, and with the block removed from the expansion, and using wet steam, we averaged 16 knots for the trip; the fastest I've seen a trawler move. When we arrived we found the doctor await-

ing us on the pilot boat. His diagnosis was that the patient was suffering from a burst appendix, peritonitis had set in, and if his life was to be saved an operation was required. The nearest hospital where the operation could be performed was at Hammerfest, about 40 miles away, and the doctor suggested that Jack should be moved to the pilot boat for the journey. Skipper Latham declined the offer. If speed was essential we could cover the distance in half the time it would take the pilot boat. So, with the doctor on board, we set off.

After putting doctor and patient ashore we didn't return to Bear Island. Just fifty miles from Hammerfest, we shot the gear on Cape Bank and found very good fishing. A week later we were back in Hammerfest. Jack had recovered from the surgery and returned to Grimsby with us. From that trip on it was always Jim Latham's boast that he was the only skipper from the Humber ports who had taken a man to sea with his appendix in, and brought him home without them. The last time I saw him alive was on the afternoon of the day before he sailed on his last trip. We played solo all afternoon at the Cyclist's Club. I was out of a ship at the time, and before we parted we arranged that I would await his return, and sign on mate with him the next trip.

It wasn't to be though. Jim took ill while at sea, and though he completed the fishing and brought the ship home, he was in a bad way on arrival. Bringing him ashore on a stretcher, one of the ambulance men slipped on the slime on the floor of the fish market, causing Jim to fall on his head. He passed quietly away in hospital the next day.

It was his wish that when his end came he

should be buried at sea, and when his ship, Northern Princess, sailed it carried the weighted casket. Skipper Jimmy Nunn took the ship away and conducted the sombre burial service far out in the wastes of the North Atlantic, and the remains of the man who had spent so much of his life on those desolate waters was confined to his final resting place in their deeps.

Are you superstitious? In common with many seamen, I am.

After the burial service Northern Princess proceeded to the Greenland fishing grounds. En route, one of the crew remarked, "Old Jim will want a ship and crew now." That same trip the Norman and her crew were lost. Shortly afterwards Northern Princess parted both warps, and the set of gear that had been used on Jim's last trip was lost. Had he claimed his fishing gear?

In an occupation where every trip was a gamble, and every winter claimed some of the players, it is hardly surprising that the fishermen were a superstitious lot, and that they and their women observed a large number of taboos. Taboos that had been handed down from generation to generation from the early days of the smacks. Maybe even from the days when Peter cast his nets on the Sea of Galilee. On the fishing ground you never left an unattended broom on the deck. It would sweep your luck away. More likely someone would trip over it in the dark, or it would get washed away. Pigs and rabbits were considered to be unlucky, and if you did refer to them you called them long ears or curly tails. You never looked at the new moon through glass; such indiscretion would surely bring misfortune for the

entire lunar cycle, and you never whistled when the gear was down; that would call up the wind.

To sail on a Good Friday was unlucky, and to leave dock on the 13th of any month would invite disaster. The Howe sailed on 13 November 1931, and look what happened to her. When you returned home from sea you always entered the house by the same door as you had left, and when you set out to rejoin your ship for the next voyage you kept your eyes straight ahead facing the docks, and never looked back. If you did you might not be turned into a pillar of salt, but some equally unpleasant mishap would occur. If you found you had forgotten some item of sea gear on no account should you return for it; that would tempt providence. One young mate I know did return home unexpectedly shortly after leaving, and found the taxi driver who had driven him down to the dock making love to his wife. Just who was unlucky, the mate or the taxi driver, is a matter for speculation.

On your way down to the dock if a black cat crossed your path that was a good omen; the voyage would be a success. On the other hand, if you met a nun, a parson, or a cross-eyed women, that was bad news. The only way to remedy the situation was to return home by a different route, and set out again. On no account must your wife or mother wash your dirty clothes on the day you sailed. If she did you wouldn't return.

There were many more rituals to be followed. No doubt all of them silly superstitions and old wives tales. Nothing to them really, and no one believed in them. Not in these days of electronic navigation systems and computerised position fixing. The witches and trolls, and their potions, spells and curses belong to an age long passed away. But what if there was something in them? It cost nothing to be on the safe side, just in case. Not when so much was at stake. Far better to be safe than sorry. You never know, do you?

Preparing to shoot the gear. A fisherman chops the trawl clear of ice on arrival at the fishing grounds.

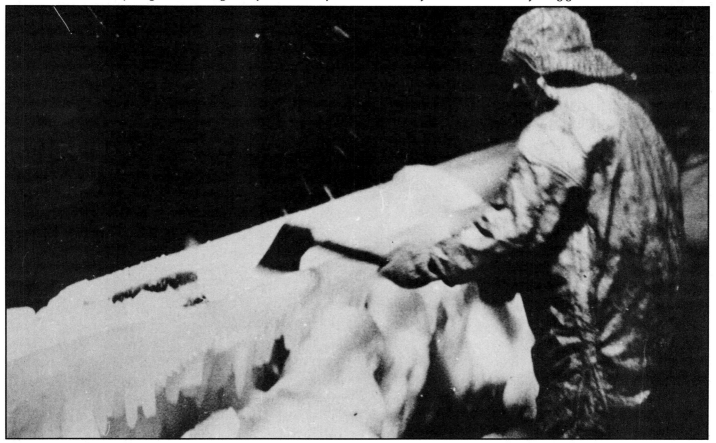

Normal Artic fishing conditions. Pitch dark and freezing cold. The trawl has just been hauled and shot away again. The first man in the fish pounds prepares to start gutting (Hull Docks Museum).

Chapter Eight

THE BIRTH OF AN ISLAND

The Westman Isles are a group of islands that climb out of the sea a few miles off the south coast of Iceland. For the most part they are little more than large rocks with steep, almost vertical sides that tower several hundred feet above sea level, and they stand like sentinels guarding the eastern approaches to Faxa Bay and Reykjavik.

Only one of the islands is inhabited. Vestmannaeyjar supports a thriving community whose living is derived from the fish shoals that abound in the surrounding waters, and the large fish processing plant that provides employment for most of those islanders that don't man the fishing boats.

According to the 'Arctic Pilot', and other works on geography and geology, these isles and rocks are of volcanic origin, formed from the lava and ash that erupted through the earth's crust when internal pressure caused a rift in a weak spot. As the average fisherman is neither a geologist nor an ecologist this explanation would be of little interest to him.

If asked to hazard a guess as to how the Westman Isles were formed he would probably suggest, knowing the fury of the gales that blow in this area, that they were once joined to the mainland, and that over the centuries the wind and sea had eroded the land, just leaving these extremities of hard rock

standing. If pressed, he would probably express scepticism of the geologist's explanation, and offer the example of land erosion at Spurn Point, and the Yorkshire coast to substantiate his viewpoint. That was before the events of 13th November 1963.

We were working about fifteen miles east of the main island, just on the deep side of the hundred fathom line. We had a couple of days good fishing, but that day the fish took off, the previous three or four hauls producing nothing. It seemed later as if the fish, by some uncanny means, knew that something was going to happen, and decided to leave the area.

It was a fine night, dark and clear, and the Northern Lights were putting on quite a show. There was no perceptible tidal wave said to usually be associated with sub-sea volcanic activity, and staring out of the wheelhouse window over the deserted fore deck, the first indication I had that something remarkable and extremely unusual was happening, was a patch of orange glow low on the horizon in the direction of the islands. I paid scant attention to it, believing that it was the reflection from the deck lights of some trawler just below the horizon.

We pulled the gear aboard just as dawn was breaking. There was no fish in the net and we headed westward in search of a more productive ground. As it grew lighter I could see a huge pillar of smoke rising, the base of the dense, black plume tinged with a ruddy glow. Black dust, wind borne, was settling on the deck and reducing visibility, and an acrid smell of sulphur was very noticeable. My first thought at the time was that an oil tanker was on fire, but the V.H.F. radio was tuned in on the distress frequency, and no distress calls had been broadcast.

We headed towards the smoke, and as we got closer the orange glow became more pronounced. Nearer still, it looked through the binoculars as if the sea was on fire. Huge bursts of orange coloured fire flared up one minute, only to be blotted out by dense, black smoke the next. Smoke and sparks shot upwards and formed a column that seemed miles high. By now the ash and dust carpeting the foredeck was inches deep, and as we passed the conflagration less than a mile away, the men lining the rail to watch the spectacle could feel the heat of the inferno on their faces, and the stench of sulphur was almost overpowering. Even at that distance the roar of the eruption, and the hiss of boiling water, could be heard.

As we passed to windward we had a better view. The blaze appeared to cover an area bigger than a football pitch, and as we watched, a tongue of fire burst from the centre of the fiery mass, scattering a cascade of sparks like a giant Roman candle; a display of fireworks Guy Fawkes would have been proud of.

Throughout the following days the eruption continued, and the chatter on the V.H.F. between fishing reports was about little else. Trawlers on passage to and from the West Side were continuously passing through the area, and we received up-to-date bulletins about the volcano's progress. The wireless operators were monitoring communications between the Icelandic gunboats, and earwigging the news broadcasts on Reykjavik Radio, and from these sources we learned that a crisis situation was developing on Vestmannaeyjar. It was reported that in the main settlement the dust and ashes had almost reached the level of the upstairs window sills, and that the inhabitants were to be evacuated to the mainland.

Despite any bitterness that may have been generated by the cod wars the Icelandic gunboats were contacted, and offered the assistance of all the trawlers in the area if help was needed with the evacuation. This offer was courteously declined. I mention the above fact to demonstrate the attitude of seamen, regardless of nationality, and their desire to render any assistance possible when fellow humanity are in peril. The men that man the Icelandic gunboats have displayed this trait on many occasions, and many British trawlermen owe their lives to the skill, seamanship, and courage of these men. On one occasion the mate of the gunboat Odinn, in the rescue of the crew of the Notts County, performed an act of bravery worthy of a medal as big as Grimsby Town Hall.

About ten days after the start of the eruption, homeward bound, we passed through the islands again. The smoke was visible from twenty miles away, and the fires were still raging. It was just going dark when we passed a couple of miles to seaward, and the sight of the flickering orange coloured fire reminded me of a night spent at anchor off the Bar Light Vessel, watching Liverpool burn after an air raid.

I passed the place often over the next three or four years. Gradually the fires subsided and the last wisps of smoke disappeared. For a long time, each occasion I saw the newborn island it seemed to have grown a bit bigger. Then, one summer, patches of green began to show. By the spring of 1967 the new island covered an area of one square mile, and at its highest point was five hundred and sixty feet above sea level, and nearly a thousand feet above the seabed. In 1965, the Icelandic Government christened its new baby Surts Island, after Surtur, the fire god of Icelandic mythology. You'll find it on Admiralty charts just a few miles southwest of Vestmannaeyjar under the name of Surtsey.

Nowadays, life on the island has returned to normal, and a research station has been set up on Surtsey by American and Icelandic geologists, but none of the inhabitants will forget that night in November 1963 when Mother Earth gave birth to an island.

An island is born. The early stages of the eruption which formed Surtsey photographed from a trawler in the vicinity.

Surtsey after the fires had died down. Some of the other Westman Isles can be seen in the background.

Chapter Nine

A CASE OF EXPLOITATION

As 1949 drew to a close changes in the fishing industry began to occur, all of them detrimental to the trawlermen's interests. Some of these changes were evolutionary and beyond their control, but others were imposed on them by the trawler owners who were united in the conviction that if a fisherman wasn't working every hour that God sent, he wasn't earning his keep. These imposed conditions could, should, and would have been resisted and rejected had the men working on the trawlers been an organized work force. But how is it possible for men to form a united front when at any one time ninety per cent of them are isolated, and scattered all over the Arctic?

In Britain an extensive trawler-building programme had put bigger, faster, more powerful ships on the fishing grounds, greatly increasing catching capacity. The Russian trawler fleet had expanded on a massive scale, and the number of Icelandic, Faroese, Norwegian, German and French trawlers operating in northern waters was increasing.

This increase in fishing activity began to deplete the fish stocks, and dip and fill came to an end. While good fishing was still to be had, rather than fish being everywhere, it had to be searched for. When you did find a fish shop the number of trawlers on the ground ensured that it rarely lasted for more than a day or two. Then you were searching again, and the size of the catches brought home by individual boats began to fall.

It is reasonable to suppose that with smaller catches the trawlerman's workload would be reduced, but this was not so. In fact, the opposite applied. Regardless of the size of the catch, the work involved in preparing the fishing gear remains unchanged, and with smaller amounts of fish being caught the ship spent less time laid with the gear aboard while deckloads of fish were being cleared. Consequently there was time for a greater number of hauls, and the amount of fish in the net makes little difference to the effort required to haul and shoot it. Further, as the gear was being towed along the bottom for longer periods of time, there was a corresponding increase in the amount of repair work on it. Hence, despite smaller catches, the men were still working an eighteen hour day.

In 1949, the control price regulations were abolished, and the fish was sold by auction on the quayside, supply and demand determining the selling price. This, together with reducing fish stocks, removed the necessity for the fish to be headed at sea. The trawler owners reasoned that because we no longer had to head the fish we had less work to do, and promptly cut down the size of the deck crews. In the Northern Boats the number of deck-hands was reduced by four, from eighteen to fourteen.

But with the end of controlled prices the quality of the fish offered for auction had to be taken into account if the best price was to be realized, and as soon as the ships were running with the smaller crews, shelving was introduced. Shelving is a method of stowing fish that requires every fish to be handled. Each shelf consists of boards covered with a bed of ice on which a single layer of fish is packed. For comparison, a pound of fish stowed in bulk will contain three shelves, but when shelving, that same pound will contain about fifteen shelves, and will hold about half as much fish. The extra labour involved is at least as great as that needed to head the fish, but the men taken away when heading stopped were never returned. There was more injustice to come.

Although individual catches were inclined to be a bit smaller, due to the increased size of the home fleet, and a larger number of foreign vessels dumping their catches at the Humber ports, a greater amount of fish was being put on the market. Quick freezing was in its infancy, and during the summer months saturation point was reached. Perfectly good fish was unable to find buyers, and was converted to fish meal for animal food. During one three month period from the beginning of June 1950, when I was mate of the Northern Pride, in three trips we put ashore about 10,000 ten stone kits of cod from Bear Island, and over ninety per cent of the fish went for fish meal. In return for flogging my guts out for three months, my remuneration was less than I

might have expected had I been employed as an office boy. The trawler owners introduced two measures to counter this situation, and defend their interests, both of which crucified the men that caught the fish. First, they imposed a quota system limiting the amount each British trawler could land on any one trip. Northern Pride's quota was 2,360 kits. The purpose of the quota was to regulate downwards the amount of fish on the market to a level the trade could accommodate, and in no way was it an attempt to conserve fish stocks. Quotas never will, and never can, conserve the fisheries, for the simple reason that present day and future fishermen, will react to those quotas in exactly the same way we did. Compelled to bring home less fish than they can catch, they will ensure that the fish they do bring home is the type and size that will command the highest price. They will still have the same number of hauls they would have had before the imposition of the quota, and the smaller fish that they would have landed will be thrown back into the sea. As many, or more, immature fish will be slaughtered, and skippers and owners will devise means of falsifying records and fishing logs.

When Governments are serious about introducing conservation measures they will approve legislation to drastically reduce catching power, and prohibit fishing on the breeding grounds of endangered stocks for extended periods of time. The cost of paying compensation to the owners of decommissioned boats, and effectively policing the closed fishing grounds would be heavy, but there is no other way. Perhaps they might set a precedent and channel some of the compensation towards the men whose living has been taken away, and whose loss is at least as great as that of the ship owners.

With the imposition of the quota the owners cut the deck crews again. Our fourteen deckhands were reduced to ten, making the total ship's compliment twenty men. At the end of the summer, when strawberries and salads disappeared from the menu, the fish buyers returned and there was a market for our product. The quota was lifted and we could land as much fish as we could catch, but we didn't get back the four deckies that had been lopped off the crew when the quotas were introduced.

We were now operating the ships with what were virtually skeleton crews, but another penny pinching economy was loaded onto the broad backs of the trawlermen. The Northern Boats had never carried a decky-learner, it being accepted that at the speed we ran the gear up and down, and the atrocious weather we worked in, the job was too dangerous for other than highly skilled personnel. That policy was changed, and a learner, paid a fraction of the amount a qualified man was entitled to, was signed on. Everyone has to learn, and had the decky-learner been an addition to the crew the practice would have been reasonable, but when the young lad signed the articles an experienced crew member was discharged, thus adding to the workload of those men remaining. Over a period of a few months the size of the crews were arbitrarily reduced by 45 per cent, with no corresponding increase in pay for the extra work done by men already working inhuman hours.

The second measure the trawler owners adopted raised little comment at the time, but can only be described as legalized robbery as far as the fishermen were concerned. They imposed minimum prices at the quayside auctions, and when fish failed to reach this minimum price it was automatically consigned to the fish meal works, the price paid for it being little more than pennies. But consider what was happening. The trawler owning companies also owned the fishmeal plants, and you don't need a degree in economics to be able to calculate a reserve price for the fish below which it would be more profitable to convert it to animal food.

Sometimes, in a period of glut, whole catches failed to realize the minimum price and were carted off to the fishmeal works. Often in these circumstances, the wholesale fish merchants would have been prepared to take the fish at a slightly reduced price - a price greater than that paid for fishmeal - but that was never allowed. From the trawler owners' point of view, what they lost on the roundabout they gained on the swings, and the unfortunate trawlermen, whose remuneration depended on the price the fish was sold for, were the losers. But as one owner was heard to comment "If they have too much money they only get drunk."

Coping with the work with these tiny crews made further inroads into the very limited time the men had for relaxation. Bridge watches had to be maintained on passage, and as the crew cutbacks had deleted the daymen, the only way to get the fishing gear prepared and rigged alongside, and all the other necessary tasks completed before the ship arrived on the fishing grounds, was to introduce field days. One day all hands would turn to, just leaving one man on the bridge to act as helmsman. By working from breakfast till dark most of the work could be done, but it meant everyone putting in a sixteen to twenty hour day. As mate I tried to arrange the field day so that it fell when I had the bridge watch from 0300 till 0730. After breakfast I would be working until 1800, with just half an hour off for dinner. Then, after tea, I would take the bridge watch from 1830 till 2300, a twenty hour day. This was the equivalent of adding another day's fishing to the trip, but as no fish were caught it was extra work that was not paid for.

On the fishing ground working with the smaller crew was even more punishing. Allowing for the watch below, where we previously had fifteen men on deck, now we had only nine, if you count the decky-learner as a man. With two men down the fishroom to shelf the fish, that left six men and a boy to do the gutting. Being able to gut fish faster than the fishroom men could shelf it, when the last fish was gutted we all had to drop down the morgue to help out. One six hour watch every day, from midnight till 0630, the Old Man would turn in for a nap, and the mate would be on the bridge, so we lost another man from the deck, although when fishing was heavy, most skippers denied themselves the luxury of going to bed and stayed on the bridge till their knees swelled up like tree trunks, and only willpower kept them going.

About twelve days after fishing operations started, when we hauled the gear for the last time, every man would be completely knackered, but someone had to take the first homeward bound steaming watch. I contend that at that stage of the trip the watchkeepers were too exhausted to meet any reasonable criteria regarding ability to guarantee safe navigation in dangerous waters. The surprising thing is that there were not more casualties than did actually occur.

The aforesaid privations that were inflicted on the fishermen, though immoral, were legal and completely in accordance with the archaic laws which regulate the lives of seamen, and govern the conditions they work in, but some of the practices the trawler owners indulged in to add a few bob to their already considerable fortunes were questionable, and it is doubtful if they would have stood up to close scrutiny.

Take the Ghost Train for instance. Every trawlerman was aware of its operation, but was powerless to interfere with its running. It was just another cross he had to bear, and could do nothing about if he wanted to keep his job. Every trawler owning company on the docks operated a subsidiary wholesale fish merchanting business. Each time a trawler discharged its catch, in the early hours before the auction started, a truckload of the best fish would be removed from the quayside, and taken to the owner's fish merchanting premises. This fish never appeared on the landing tally, and its value was never added to the vessel's grossing, so the crew, whose remuneration included a tiny share of the value of the catch, were robbed of their share of this fish. Any mate who enquired as to the destination of his departing fish would be told blandly, "Oh, its going to the fish house. If any of the crew want a fry they can pop in to collect it." Whether that crew would be allowed to pop in and come away with fifty or sixty boxes of prime fish is left to the reader's imagination, but the odds are that any mate foolish enough to raise a stink would find himself stood on the corner looking for another job.

Just how much fish the Ghost Train transported from the market every morning is anybody's guess, and the amount purloined from each trawler was probably in direct proportion to the size of its catch. The loss to each crew member on any individual trip was insignificant, but taken right across the fish market, over a whole year, the fiddle amounted to grand larceny. At a conservative estimate:-

Assume that 100 distant water trawlers operated from Grimsby, that each trawler made fifteen trips a year, and that the Ghost Train collected an average of 50 kits of fish from each trawler each trip. The total amount of fish spirited away would be :

15 X 50 X 100 = 75,000 kits of fish.

Taking an average price of £5 per kit, the value of this fish is £375,000. I have often wondered if it was ever included in any tax return. And we haven't included the hundreds of near and middle water trawlers, all of whom paid tribute to the Ghost Train.

Out of work, I accepted the offer of a mate's berth in one of Bacon's ships, the Valmont, with Skipper Ted Cave. After a fourteen day trip to Faroe Bank we landed as good a trip as you could expect for the class of ship, about 600 kit of cod and haddock. Bacon owned, among other dockland enterprises, a fish merchant business that traded under the name of Dolphin Fish Company, and in the course of the trip I heard stories about the extravagant amount of fish the Dolphin carried away before the start of the sales.

6 a.m. one morning found me standing on the fish market alongside the Valmont's catch. Market forecasts were good, so was the fish. I had no worries.

Bacon's manager walked round and inspected the trip.

"Nice trip, Mr. Mate," he said, "nip up to the canteen and have a cuppa. I'll be here till after the sales."

I was back from the cafe in five minutes flat. A couple of labourers were putting the finishing touches to loading about fifteen boxes of our best shelf haddock aboard a flat barrow.

"That's the second load they've taken," one of Valmont's deckhands told me.

On being confronted the stage foreman came up with the usual "They're going to the Dolphin. When you want a fry ...."

"Do I, and the Skipper, get paid for them?" I countered.

"You'll have to talk to the gaffer about that. I'm only a workman," he said, seeming surprised that authority was being challenged, and wishing to be distanced from possible trouble.

"I will," I replied.

Later that morning, while on my way to the office to settle, I bumped into the mate of the Sleight's ship that had discharged her catch next to Valmont. From him I learned that his fish had sold for £3,500. We had been fishing within sight of each other all the trip, and we had about 100 kit of fish more, so I expected our trip to have sold for about £4,000 .

At the time I'm writing about the skipper was

paid 10 per cent, and the mate 7.125 per cent of the ship's net earnings, less the cost of their food. On settling we were presented with two papers. On one the details of all the chargeable expenses were stated, and the price the fish had realized at the auction. The other gave details of earnings and deductions - store bill, bond, food charge, allotment and the like. According to one sheet the Valmont's fish had sold for just over £2,000 and the expenses for the voyage were £1,800. My personal account was written in handwriting that resembled a doctor's prescription, and was unreadable. Barely decipherable figures were laid alongside of illegible items. The bottom line told me I owed the company £ 3.

A single man, I sent no allotment home, and I had no store bill to pay. The only deductions from my pay should have been the food charge and a couple of pounds for a bottle of bonded scotch and a carton of cigarettes. According to Bacon's cashier, I had done a fortnights work, landed a good trip of fish, and owed him three pounds for my trouble. I was being classed as an idiot and being taken for a ride. I determined to do something about it.

Leaving the office, I went straight home and studied the accounts, comparing the figures with those of the big distant water trawlers I usually shipped in. Valmont's expenses were listed as higher per day than those of the Northern boats, ships three times as big, that burnt more than twice the amount of coal, and carried double the crew.

I picked up the phone, dialled Bacon's number, and asked for the cashier. "I'm not happy with my settling sheet," I told him.

"It's Nicklin moaning about his settling," I heard

him say to someone in the background, then he reeled off a list of figures at a speed an accountant might have been able to follow. I couldn't.

"I'm still not happy," I said, "and I thought I'd better let you know that in five minutes I'll be on my way to the Board of Trade to get their accountant to explain it to me."

Ten seconds silence then, "Don't be hasty, Mr. Nicklin. Ah, yes. One of the clerks has made a mistake. If you come down you have some money to draw."

Half an hour later, when I entered the general office, the typewriter ceased its chatter, and the hubbub of commercial activity was replaced by an unnatural silence. I could almost feel several pairs of eyes on me.

"This is where the mistake was made," the cashier said, showing me some scribble on the back of a fish tally, "If you give me back your settling sheet I'll make a new one out."

I stowed the £70 or so he pushed across the desk in my hip pocket, and kept a tight hold on the settling sheet. It seemed important to him.

"Aren't you forgetting something," I said.

"What's that?" he asked.

"This morning about thirty kit of shelf haddock was moved to the Dolphin by your workmen. Haddock made over £6 a kit this morning. I want paying for them or this settling sheet goes to the Marine Superintendent with my complaint," I told him.

"You'll have to see Mr. Bacon," he said, and moved to one of the doors, tapped, entered and closed the door behind him.

He was back in five minutes, and grudgingly

pushed another £20 my way as if it was his own money he was parting with. Maybe it was, I don't know. As I left the office the typewriter started up again, and the chatter resumed.

There is a big difference between owing £3 and being £90 to the good. About three o'clock that afternoon, I had just finished eating lunch when the phone rang. It was Bacon's ships husband.

"There'll be a fresh mate going in the Valmont next trip, Mr. Nicklin," he said, "The gaffer says you're a trouble maker."

That was the most blatant mistake I ever came across, and concerned an individual and one specific company, but the trawlermen were often cheated across the board. Wherever money was concerned, the owners were never content until they got it all. That characteristic eventually led to the total decimation of the industry at the end of the Cod Wars.

The fishermen didn't enjoy many perks, and the few they did have were taken over by the employers as soon as they looked likely to produce a few bob. The waters around the Western Isles, where many of the Fleetwood trawlers worked, abounded with prawns. Big, juicy crustaceans that were a joy to eat when boiled in seawater when first caught. These prawns were never saved as part of the catch, although it was customary for the lads to boil a few baskets to take home. Shortly after I left Fleetwood, I was told by a friend still fishing from the Lancashire port, that a small company had set up a canning plant. They began putting canisters aboard the ships for the deck crews to fill with peeled prawns, and paid £5 per can. By sacrificing a bit of sleeping time, and devoting every spare minute of the night watches to peeling prawns, the men could earn a few pounds extra spending money.

It didn't last long. The owners smelled gold, and moved in. First forbidding the crews from taking home any prawns at all, and enforcing the rule with a security booth at the dock entrance, they fitted out three ships with refrigerated fish holds, and sent them prawn fishing. One of the trawlers so converted was the Royalist, owned by Hewett Trawlers Ltd. I never heard the sequel to the enterprise. It didn't concern me directly, but there were other provocations that did.

Ever since the early days of steam trawling roes were regarded as stocker, that is, they belonged to the crew, and after the cost of the roe bags and landing charges had been deducted, the money they were sold for was shared out among the crew. The shareout never amounted to more than a few pounds. That was until the spring of 1949. One of the Northern Boats landed a big trip of cod from the Norwegian coast. She also put a considerable quantity of cod roes on the market. Control prices had recently been abolished, and the roes being the first to be landed that season, realized an extremely high price. The crew were never paid the money for them, the owners decreeing that then, and on all future trips, the roes would go in with the rest of the catch, and the deck crew would be paid ten shillings (50p) each for bagging them. The crews were up in arms over this piece of arbitrary legislation, and aboard the Northern Boats we retaliated in the only way we could. Very few roes were put on the market during the rest of that Coast season. When gutting, a quick slash of a sharp knife rendered the roes unsalable. But by the time the next coast season came round it was all forgotten, and the protest died a natural death.

Oil money was another bone of contention, and another area in which the fishermen were cheated out of what should have been theirs. When gutting the fish, the liver was separated from the guts and saved. When time allowed, the livers were boiled and the oil extracted, the proceeds being shared among the crew. What proportion the owners took I don't know, but on a big trip of cod with good livers, my share of the oil money was often between £20 and £25. Then the trawler-owners bought out the oil company, and from that time I never received more than a fiver. Oil money declined to the point were it was hardly worth the trouble saving the livers. "A drop in world prices," we were told. Somebody must have been making money out of the oil as the following example shows.

Most of the ships had egg cup boilers. These boilers looked like giant egg timers, and consisted of two cylindrical tanks, one above the other, connected by a gauge glass. The livers were boiled in the bottom tank, and after the foots has settled to the bottom of the tank water was pumped in so that the oil was floated up to the top tank. When the darker colour of the foots showed in the gauge glass the water was turned off, and the oil ran off into a storage tank. The foots were then drained overboard, and as the cross section of the gauge glass was only about two inches square, very little oil was wasted.

Aboard the Northern Boats the liver boiling plant was different to the above arrangement. The liver house was situated at deck level right at the stern, and contained four large coppers for boiling the livers in. Taps were staggered down the sides of the coppers for draining off the oil, and although water could be pumped in to bring the bottom of the oil to the level of the lowest tap a considerable amount of oil had to be left with the foots due to the large surface area of the coppers. When as much oil as possible had been skimmed off we saved the foots, running them into a separate tank. At the end of every trip the pure oil was pumped ashore, while the foot tank was emptied every second trip. One trip aboard Northern Gem, homeward bound and in the calm waters of the Norwegian fiords, we removed the lid of the foot tank and skimmed about ninety buckets of oil off the top of the foots, and poured them into the oil tank. Next trip we repeated the process. That trip the foots were pumped ashore.

When we sailed the next trip we found that hinged steel battens, secured with a heavy padlock, had been fitted across the foot tank lid, making entry to the tank impossible. Obviously, we had encroached on somebody's racket. We were told that what we had done had affected the quality of the oil, but on both trips the oil company chemist had graded the oil A.1, and the complaint had not come from the oil company, but from someone on the trawler-owners staff, and had never been raised until the foots had gone ashore. Distant water trawling was certainly not run for the benefit of the trawler crews; nor with their welfare in mind.

Chapter Ten

THE PAY - POUNDS OR PEANUTS

From time to time the trawler owners have shed buckets of crocodile tears. The industry is tottering on the verge of bankruptcy. Appeals for assistance to meet the crisis, often successful, have been made to the Government of the day. These appeals for finance: loans and grants for new buildings, grants to modernize vessels, decommissioning grants, help to cover the cost of meeting mandatory safety provisions, and the like are always stated to be made on behalf of the 'trawlermen', are made by the 'trawlermen's leaders', and when the appeal bears fruit a spokesman for the Ministry concerned announces that so many millions will be made available to assist the trawlermen over their current difficulties.

In the above context the noun 'trawlermen' always referred to the fat cats who conducted their trawling from the confines of a cosy office, whose nearest approach to a haddock occurred on their morning stroll along the fish market, and who ran their Rolls and Daimlers on the blood and sweat of the men that caught the fish.

No money from public funds ever found its way into the pockets of the men that went to sea. A case in point occurred after the Icelandic Cod Wars, when the wholesale decommissioning of the distant water trawler fleet took place. I'm not going to argue the

rights and wrongs of the dispute. I'm simply going to discuss the Cod Wars insofar as they affected the trawler crews.

That the livelihood of the Icelandic people is entirely dependent on the fish that shoal around the island's coast is universally accepted. Fish stocks in the Barents Sea had been virtually wiped out, and the same thing was beginning to happen in the waters around Iceland. A greater number of bigger, more powerful trawlers were spending more time on the fishing grounds to catch a smaller amount of the diminishing fish stock.

The Icelandic Government's first move to conserve the fisheries on which the country's economic survival depended was taken in 1953 when the three-mile fishing limit was extended to four miles. The new limit was established, not by a line running parallel to the shore and four miles offshore, but by straight lines connecting points four miles off the salient headlands, thus denying the trawlers access to all the bays and coves around the island - ground they had fished for many years. In the U.K. fishing ports there were protests and mutterings about traditional fishing rights, but the new fishing limits stuck.

As the fishing fleets, especially the Russians and British, ruthlessly and systematically swept the Barents Sea clean, catches shrunk, and there was an exodus of trawlers from that area. These trawlers flocked to Icelandic waters, and the plundering continued on an ever increasing scale.

The Icelanders reaction was logical and predictable. They pushed the limit line out to twelve miles.

The cries of anguish from the Humber trawler barons sounded almost human, and were echoed by the trawler skippers, who could see their activities curtailed, and their living endangered. Encouraged by their employers, the trawlermen ignored the new fishing limits, skirmishes with the fishery protection vessels became an everyday occurrence, and the increasing number of incidents led to the U.K. Government shaking the mailed fist at a once friendly nation, and deploying the navy to protect the trawlers, arguing that the imposition of the twelve-mile limit was a breach of international law. For the next few years what became known as the Cod Wars followed.

Iceland had no armed forces to call on, but their four or five tiny gunboats, no bigger than trawlers, were fast, highly manoeuvrable, and manned by expert seamen. They gave a surprisingly good account of themselves. Usually the presence of the naval escorts prevented them from making arrests, but they developed a highly effective tactic of towing a wire cutter across the trawl warps of any trawler they found inside the limits, thus chopping the trawler's gear away. The trawlermens' defence was to work in groups of three, one ship trawling, with the other two keeping on each quarter, trying to prevent the gunboat getting at the trawl warps. This reduced fishing time by two thirds, but still, hardly a

day passed that some trawler didn't have her gear cut away.

The gunboats were not the only inconvenience the fishermen had to bear. Throughout the winters, fear of arrest denied them the shelter of the fiords, and when requiring stores or repairs, they could no longer make use of the facilities of the Icelandic ports, and had to make the long trip to harbours in the Faroe Isles.

Taking her case to N.A.T.O., Iceland presented an unarguable case in favour of her conservation measures, but despite winning the vote the Cod Wars continued. Matters came to a head when Iceland finally broke off diplomatic relations with the Britain, and declared a 200 mile fishing limit round the island. This limit fenced off every fishing ground in Icelandic waters, and at the talks that followed Iceland stipulated a maximum tonnage of fish that could be taken from those waters, and offered all the countries, including Britain, who had traditionally fished in Icelandic waters, a negotiated share of that quota. The British Government, advised by the trawler owners, who were never satisfied unless they got the whole cake, declined the offer, and hostilities on the fishing grounds continued.

But although Iceland had no armed forces, she had one ace in the hole to play. N.A.T.O. had a base at Keflavic, manned by the Americans, which was crucial to the early warning system in the North Atlantic. In exchange for the base facilities the U.S.A. had guaranteed to defend Icelandic sovereignty. The Americans received an ultimatum: get British warships out of Icelandic waters, or get the hell out of Keflavic.

Washington leaned on Whitehall, and the navy withdrew to home waters.

The trawler owners, kicking and screaming, had to accept defeat. But for their inherent greed they could have accepted a small quota sufficient to have sustained a limited fishery. In the event they came away from the dispute with nothing. Subsequently Russia, Norway, Canada, and Greenland extended the fishing limits around their Arctic coasts, and imposed quotas on the amount that could be taken. There was nowhere left to plunder. The goose that laid the golden egg was dead, and wholesale decommissioning of the trawlers followed.

The 'trawlermens leaders' put their money into other enterprises and retired to their country seats, leaving behind a legacy of dilapidated, almost deserted fish docks, clusters of boarded up shops and business premises, and a small army of unemployed men.

When the trawlers were decommissioned a benign government paid the owners fifteen million pounds compensation to help them make ends meet, and keep the wolf from the door. The men that had manned the ships, men who had lost their livelihood, many of whom would never work again, received not one penny for their loss, not even a token redundancy payment.

Surely what is good for the goose is good for the gander, and the men that had spent so many years at sea in the ships deserved a better deal than this final kick in the teeth before being consigned to the scrap heap. Francis Quarles (1592 -1644) wrote:

"Our God and soldiers we like adore
Ev'n at the brink of danger; not before.

After deliverance, both alike requited.
Our Gods forgotten and our soldiers slighted."

Quarles's verse is appropriate to the treatment doled out to the fishermen at the cessation of the Cod Wars.

More than once, usually at times when a spell of bad weather has halted fishing operations for two or three weeks, and fish is realizing sky high prices at the quayside, articles in the local and national press have dwelled on the fabulous amount of money the trawlermen are reputed to earn. These articles always refer to some one-off record breaking voyage, but the price of fish is regulated by supply and demand, and when fish makes these high prices it is because most of the trawlers have little, or nothing, to sell.

The fallacy that the men were paid big money was encouraged by the owners. It helped recruitment, and ensured a pool of new entrants who could eventually be trained as replacement crews. These young lads soon discovered that the job was not all it was cracked up to be, and the drop-out rate was high. It also lent justification to the high price of fish at the retail end of the chain. Even when there was a glut at the ports, the price in the shops never came down.

Without doubt the men themselves, having to squeeze a month's living into the two days they were ashore, and having a month's pay to dispose of to help them do it, added credence to the myth, and earned them the misnomer 'two day millionaires'.

The men did earn very high wages, but they were never paid a proper rate for the work they did. They also earned the right to a humane length of working day, an adequate amount of time to sleep off their fatigue, overtime and premium rates for weekend and Bank Holiday work, a reasonable spell in dock between trips, a leave system comparable with that won by their counterparts in the Merchant Navy, meaningful compensation when they were crippled or killed on the job, and a decent pension when age or infirmity put an end to their seagoing days; conditions that are taken for granted by almost every other group of workers in a civilized society, but were denied the trawlermen.

There was very little difference between the rates of pay of deckhands, firemen, cooks, wireless operators, and 2nd engineers, so I'll use the last complete year I sailed as deckhand as an example. For the entire 1948/49 tax year I was employed as decky on the Northern Duke with Skipper Bill Woods. I made fourteen trips, all of them to Bear Island or the Barents Sea, and spent a total of 324 days at sea. I had one trip off with a damaged arm.

That year Northern Duke was the top money earning trawler working from Grimsby, grossing close on £120,000, and in considering my remuneration you should bear in mind that many trawlers earned half as much, or less, than Northern Duke. No deckhand earned more, most earned considerably less.

My gross pay for the year was less than £1,200, and comprised a basic weekly wage of £7.50, poundage at the rate of £6 per £1,000 of the ship's gross earnings, and a share of the liver money that averaged about £10 a trip. Taking average grossing at £8,000 per trip, the breakdown is as follows:

Basic Wage: 48 weeks at £7.50 per week = £(48 X 7.5) = **£360**
Poundage: £(14 X 8 X 6)   = **£672**
Liver Money: £(14 X 10)   = **£140**
Total gross earnings for the year   = **£1,172**

That might seem a lot of money for those days, but let us calculate an hourly rate:

I spent 324 days at sea, and assuming a working day of 12 hours when on passage, and 18 hours when fishing, if we take an average of 15 hours a day for the period we won't be far out. Then, if we divide the amount earned by the number of hours worked, we will get an approximate hourly rate.

Hours worked = 324 X 15 = 4,860 hours and
Hourly rate = £(1172/4860) = £0. 24 per hour

Twenty four pence an hour for working an 18 hour day for most of the time, a seven day week, and in conditions of extreme danger and discomfort, can hardly be described as a fabulous rate of pay for highly skilled operatives in the top ship in the port. Most other trawlermen worked just as hard, for as many hours, for half that amount of money. Remember too, that to work in the Arctic climate the men had to spend about six or seven pounds a trip on sea gear. A pair of thigh boots lasted about three trips if you were lucky, an oilskin two trips, and I used to wear out six pairs of gutting gloves and two pairs of woollen mittens each trip.

Now let us look at the top of the tree, and consider the skipper's earnings. Very few trawler skippers went to sea for the full twelve months. While at sea they put in even more time than the outrageous hours their crews had to work. This, coupled with the mental stress they were under, dictated that they stopped off for at least two trips a year, usually a break in the summer, and another at Christmas, to recharge their batteries, if they were not to degenerate into mental and physical wrecks.

At the time we are talking about the skipper was paid 10 per cent of the net earning of his ship. Assuming our skipper made twelve trips, averaging £8,000 a trip, and ship's expenses of £2,800 a trip, we can get a close approximation of the year's pay.

Vessel's Gross Earnings: £(8000 X 12)	= £96,000
Vessel's Expenses: £(2800 X 12)	= £33,600
Net Earnings	= £62,400
Skippers Share: 10% of net earnings	= £6,240
Charge for food at 8 per trip £96	
Approximate Annual Gross Pay	= £6,144

This was on one of the top boats in the port during a year at the height of the boom. These are the earnings of a man who was a peer among his fellows. When you think about what he had to do to earn that money, the years he slaved in the Arctic gaining the knowledge and experience necessary to make those earnings possible, and the amount of icy water he'd wrung from his seaboot stockings during those learning years, perhaps the pay doesn't seem so generous. Bear in mind too, that his only security of tenure to the job was dependent on being able to produce similar grossing on future trips, thus keeping the owners happy. Three consecutive bad trips and he would be stood on the corner with those other unfortunates whose luck had run out, or who had offended some member of the fish dock aristocracy, and who were lucky if they made two trips a year relieving.

If these out of works came home with good catches when they got the chance to take a ship away as relief skipper they would be offered more work, but the dice was loaded against them. Those skippers that could lay title to a regular ship knew the times of the year when fish would be scarce, and when the weather would so severe that fishing operations would be hampered, and naturally, these were the times they took their break. With competition to gain and retain a command so keen, who can blame them? The whole job was a case of dog eat dog, which was another reason the men were never able to organize themselves into forming a united front.

As for being the best paid members of the work force, the truth is that we were probably the worst paid. Had a factory hand been allowed to work the hours we were forced to work, in a couple of years he would have been able to buy the factory.

Alan Adams sailed as wireless operator on the Kingston Boats from Hull throughout the boom years, and illustrated on the next page are two of his pay slips, one a reasonably good trip, and the other not so good on Kingston Chrysoberyl, both voyages to Iceland.

As a 'sparks' poundage was the same as that of a deckhand, we can easily calculate the decky's hourly rate of pay which includes his £7.50 weekly wage.

Assuming both trips were 22 days duration, his gross hourly rate would be about 22 pence and 13.25

pence per hour respectively, giving an average of 17.6 pence an hour for both trips.

I offer these documents to destroy once and for all the myth, that we received fabulous wages for doing a cushy number. In fact the reverse applied. We were grossly overworked, and disgracefully underpaid.

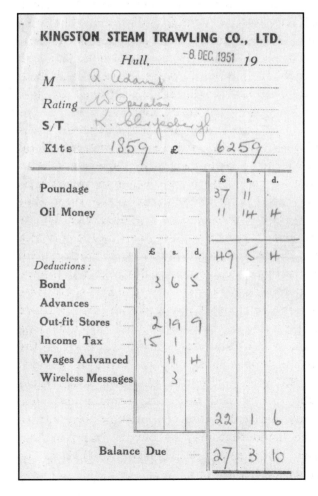

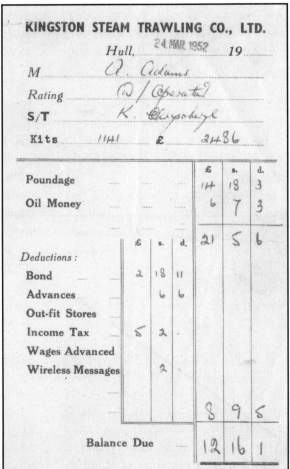

Chapter Eleven

THE FOOD

In every country on the globe, in every walk of life, the denizens spend a considerable part of their wakeful hours hunting or shopping for food, preparing and cooking it, and finally feasting on it. As in many circles, the dining table in the saloon or messdeck is the focal point of social activity aboard a trawler. Here, after enjoying a meal, especially on passage, the men will compare the relative qualities of the females whose favours they had sampled on their last spell ashore, the miseries they had endured under previous skippers, or maybe the antics they proposed to get up to on their next time in dock. So perhaps a chat about the feeding on trawlers is appropriate.

During the war most foodstuffs were strictly rationed to the general population, but rationing never applied to the trawlermen when they were on board ship, and only partially when they were on shore between trips. When a trawler docked the men collected a ration card from the local Food Office. This card entitled them to one weeks rations, and as they were only in dock for thirty-six hours, they were about four times as well off as a shore worker. Their families enjoyed another perk in the 'grub stakes'. At the end of each fishing trip it was customary for each crew member to take home a bass of fish which often weighed a couple of stone or more. This fish was always selected from the trawler's last haul, so was always in the freshest possible condition, and its quality was far superior to anything that could be bought in the shops. The men also brought home prawns, crabs, lobsters, and shellfish; delicacies that could not be obtained for love nor money away from the fishing ports.

While most fishermen had scant regard for the seafood they were in daily contact with, the local farmers looked on them as a prize. Once contact was made the farmers were always eager to barter eggs, chickens, meat and dairy produce for what they considered the gourmet's fare the fishermen had to offer. As both farmer and fisherman had access to a surplus of the commodity he was bartering, each believed he was getting a good deal. As a consequence, the families of farmers and fishermen ate well.

The Department of Trade and Industry, or Board of Trade as it was then called, laid down detailed minimum victualling scales which set out the amount and type of foodstuffs that must be provided for all seafarers, including fishermen, when those foodstuffs can be obtained at reasonable cost; and when any particular item is unobtainable, substitutes are listed that may be put on board in lieu. However, these scales were never applied to the distant water trawlers.

I have no love for the trawler owners, who were not averse to exploit the fishermen in every possible way to add an extra pound or two to their bank balances, but even these men seemed to agree that if men were to work an eighteen hour day in Arctic conditions, they needed a more substantial diet than bread and jam. Hence, we were well fed and watered.

On one occasion when I was waiting in Boston's Grimsby office to sign on a ship, a cook had ordered some item of provisions the previous trip and it had not been delivered. On complaining to the ship's runner he was told he could not have that particular item. Taking the matter further, the cook went upstairs and complained to Mr. Fred Parkes Jnr. who was Managing Director at the time. While I was stood in the office, Mr. Parkes entered. "What's all this about", he snarled at the unfortunate runner, "I've told you before. Feed the bastards." Enough said. I spent a couple of years on Boston's ships and was always well fed.

While there was a considerable difference in the feeding in the ships owned by different companies, and even in ships owned by the same company, I believe that this difference was mainly due to the ability of the cooks rather than to the amount of food that was put aboard. In every group of workers you will find members who are good, bad, or indifferent, and one or two who stand head and shoulders above their compatriots. I suppose trawler cooks are no different in this respect.

From 1947, when I moved to Grimsby, until 1969 when I left that port, I spent almost all my time afloat aboard the biggest class of distant water trawler, the snappers as they were known. These ships were the hardest worked, but because they earned the most money berths in them were the most sought after, hence their crews tended to be drawn from the most experienced men. This applied to cooks as well as to other ratings.

Most of the cooks I sailed with were artists at their job. All of them could put a meal on the table that would not have disgraced the Savoy. They performed their art in a galley measuring about twelve feet by seven on a coal or oil burning stove, and regardless of whether the ship was being tossed and thrown about on the fishing ground, or being driven into a head gale force wind with sea to match, the hot meal was always ready in time to fit in with the rigorous time schedule demanded by operational requirements. Sometimes the trawler would be bouncing about with such violence that even the seasoned seadogs on deck had difficulty keeping their feet, and conditions in the galley would have driven a hotel chef to the brink of suicide, but the food, accompanied by a string of curses as vehement and violent as the weather, would be brought to the table as soon as the men coming in off the deck had discarded their oilskins.

From the second day out of dock, every other day they baked bread. Not the doughy, steam-baked , sliced rubbish you buy in the supermarket, wrapped in greaseproof, and only fit for mopping up gravy and feeding to the ducks. Their bread was white, crusty stuff, light as a feather, and a joy to eat either wrapped round a slice of cheese, or plastered with butter.

Every day they cooked three substantial meals,

and put out a buffet supper to keep you going through the night, usually consisting of cheese, pickles, and the sliced remains of the luncheon joint. When the weather was particularly harsh, and there was ice on the deck, they would often leave a pan of 'shackles', a stew made with meat and vegetables, simmering on the stove, so that we could help ourselves when, and if, time allowed.

Breakfast fare on the fishing ground was always the same. As much porridge as you could eat, and a plate of fish fried like only a trawler cook can fry it. They made delicious soups, thick, meaty main course stuff that you could nearly chew, and which provided a suitable bed in the stomach to plant the luscious roast that invariably followed.

Puddings were always of the steamed or baked variety; plum, sultana, date, chocolate or apple, the size of the helpings such that would make a navvy slacken his belt, and served with as much custard as you could get on the plate without it slopping over the sides. Nor would the cook mind in the least if you did an 'Oliver Twist'. Occasionally you would be offered a milk pudding, Chinese Wedding Cake (rice) or Doll's Eyes (sago), but these were not popular, and generally reserved for the homeward passage when the heavy work was done, and stores were getting short.

They also made tasty stews, with dumplings stuffed with onions floating in them, twenty minute swimmers we called them; and 'cow pies' composed mainly of chunks of beef topped with a pastry crust an inch thick that melted in your mouth, and didn't really need the thick brown gravy that was served with it to help it down. The food placed on the trawlerman's table, while obviously containing far too high a fat content to appeal to a figure conscious socialite, or meet the approval of her dietician, or any other health fanatic, was the kind of nourishment a man needed to provide him with the energy required to endure the punishing eighteen-hour day work cycle, and to generate the body heat to fight the Arctic cold.

Where the welfare of his charges was concerned, nothing seemed too much trouble for the cook. Often we would come in off the deck for a sit down for five or ten minutes while awaiting hauling time to find a row of steaming mugs of tea ready for us, together with a plate of 'tab nabs', savoury pies, hunks of slab cake, or a freshly baked pile of hot buns straight out of the oven. And if he knew it was your birthday he'd always knock up a birthday cake.

The only service he expected in return was that the mate didn't forget him when he dished out the daily tot of rum, that the firemen kept his coal box full, that the deckies brought the breakfast fish aft when the weather was too bad for the galleyboy to go on deck, and that when he turned out in the morning the galley was as tidy as he had left it before he turned in. He also appreciated it if there was a pot of tea on the stove when he turned out.

Having sailed with so many first class chefs, it is hard to single out any particular one for special reference. It is much easier to dwell on one or two mini disasters or amusing incidents concerning them. During the war, when all categories of skilled workers were in short supply, a lot of elderly men, well over pensionable age, were coaxed back to sea to face the rigours of life afloat, when by all the rules of common decency they should have been enjoying their twilight in slippers in front of the fire. Bob, a retired trawler cook was one of these men. Well over seventy, he signed on as cook on the trawler Unita, and soon demonstrated that he had lost none of his ability when it came to shaking the pans up. In one respect, time had taken its toll, and Bob's eyesight had begun to fail. Close to mealtimes, he would scowl at the clock three or four feet away on the bulkhead, and turn to any of the lads standing nearby and ask "what time is it, Youngster?"

Bob kept the various ingredients, salt, sugar, flour and the like in a batch of identical cans on the shelf above his worktop, his failing eyesight making the labelling of the cans an unnecessary exercise. Years of practice and habit ensured he could pick out the tin he wanted in the dark.

We, the deckies, were a crowd of teenagers, fun loving and always game for a skylark when the work wasn't tying us down, but sometimes the antics we got up to were tempered with the cruelty and thoughtlessness that is synonymous with youth and immaturity. One morning when the cook was absent from his galley one of the lads shuffled his cans around. The result was a cocked up meal, sugar in the soup and salt in the custard. We idiots thought it was hilarious; the cook said never a word.

But that evening, as the crew were finishing their meal, Old Bob entered the saloon.

"How was the tea, Lads?" he asked.

"Great, Cookie," chorused the lads.

"Good," he snarled, "I'll piss in it every night, and I won't tell you what I'm putting in the gravy."

From that time on Bob was treated with the respect he was entitled to.

Christmas was a time of the year when all the family men wanted to be at home if they could afford the time off. Consequently, from the second week in December until a couple of days before New Year's Day, there was always a shortfall of labour on the fish docks. These two or three weeks were the time of the year when the hands were king. For once, the runners who had to get the ships to sea wore a worried look, smiled at you and called you by your Christian name, and made half-promises about work for the rest of the year, in their efforts to entice you into signing your name on the log book. It was the time of the year when a man could upgrade himself, and move from one of the smaller ships to a berth in one of the snappers, and if he was up to the job and his face fitted, may be retained after the holiday. I'm certain that if a runner was hard pressed enough he'd sign on a man with one leg.

I sailed as mate with Skipper George Bures on the Derby County in mid-December, bound for the Barents Sea. Our cook was 'Geordie' Brown. Geordie was a man in his early fifties. He had sailed as bosun for donkeys years, but half a lifetime spent working in wet gear, and sleeping in damp bunks, had left him crippled with rheumatism. Unable to hop about like a spring chicken any longer, he had to give up the deck work, and decided to give the galley a try. We were the sufferers.

It wasn't that Geordie was lazy. The man didn't have an idle bone in his body. When the weather was fine, and the trawl was busted, he would come out on deck, grab a needle, and help out with the repairs. I think he accepted that a braiding needle and a marline spike fitted his calloused hands better than a wooden spoon.

Mealtimes, you couldn't go round his table. The trouble was that most of the dishes he produced were uneatable. It wasn't for the want of trying - he just couldn't cook. He would stop up half the night baking three or four batches of bread, select the best one, and throw the rest overboard. The batch he saved might just be edible if you had a good set of teeth. His dumplings and duffs had the consistency of cannon balls and weighed about the same. His pastry tasted like fibre board and was as hard to digest, and had his steaks been used for soling boot they would never have worn out. I swear that no geological formation was as hard as Geordie's rock buns.

Preparing the Christmas dinner that year, Geordie excelled himself. Christmas Day morning, just after breakfast, we were hauling the gear off the Russian Arctic coast. Geordie went up to the wheelhouse to scrounge a measure of rum for the sauce.

"Don't bother me now, Geordie, you can see I'm busy," the Old Man told him, "go down and get a drop out of the jar in my cabin." Joyfully, the cook departed with a pint pot full of rum. Christmas really had come.

Needless to say, very little, if any, of the rum went into the sauce; all of it went into the cook. The two turkeys had been part cooked the night before, and needed to be finished off. One of the birds was dished up cold, and nearly raw. The other was roasted twice, and resembled a chunk of burnt coal.

I never liked to sack a man, but the alternative in this case was a plague of indigestion or stomach ulcers. Geordie had to go.

A man called Kenny West probably had the hardest runner's job on the dock. The Ross Group had a big fleet of ships, for the most part near and middle water boats, with only four or five first class distant water boats among them. It was Kenny's job to find the crews to man them. In an attempt to solve their crewing problems the company conducted a recruiting campaign in the inland towns directed at young school leavers, appealing to their sense of adventure, probably stressing the fabulous wages they could earn when they qualified as skippers, but almost certainly not telling them how much seawater they would wring from their boot stockings before they attained that rank.

Some of these young recruits spent a few weeks at school learning the rudiments of cookery, did a couple of trips as galley boy to get their sea legs, and were then thrown in at the deep end. In order to counterbalance their lack of experience, the company put large quantities of tinned foods aboard, and enough shore-baked bread to last the trip.

Northern Trawlers had no small ships, and the men in the company were all known regulars, but Christmas was a time of shortage, and one of Ross's young proteges was signed on to do the cooking on Northern Pride. The lad wasn't bad at the job either. That is for the first five or six days until the emergency stock of tinned stuff ran out. Then the rot set in. The kid couldn't bake bread, but at least he could turn out a kind of bun that was an edible substitute, and which took him half the night to bake a sufficient quantity. His biggest problem was with the puddings. Instead of having heaps of canned fruit, and a pantry stocked with convenience foods like a supermarket, he had a bin of flour, blocks of lard, and seven pound bags of sultanas and the like to play with, and he couldn't cope.

In one corner of the pantry there was a load of sago and rice. Stuff that was rarely used, was added to each trip, and allowed to accumulate. The cook found it.

We were fishing at Bear Island, and it was freezing hard. Every day we had rice pudding. First served as a milk pudding at the mid-day meal and rejected by the men, it was dried out and served with curry at tea time. Rejected again, it turned up the following day as filling in a rice tart, and finally ended up as a meal for the seagulls.

After five or six days I could no longer ignore the persistent rumbling from the crew, and the snidey remarks about Peking and slit eyes. Common sense told me it was no use leaning on the lad too hard. Perhaps he just didn't know what was expected of him. I decided to try a friendly whisper in his ear.

"This rice pudding every day", I told him, "no one's eating it. You're just wasting sugar and milk. What about doing something about it?"

"OK, John," he replied, "tomorrow I'll do something about it."

I felt pleased with myself as I told the bosun, "I think we've seen the last of the rice." Next day at lunch the cook brought out the pudding. Chinese wedding cake again. "The mate's told me to cut back on the sugar and milk so there's none in the pud-ding," he told the men, "here is a tin of milk and a bowl of sugar. Put your own on and there won't be any wasted."

After that the deckies found their own solution to the problem. That night when the cook was turned in, they raided the pantry and dumped all the rice over the side. But for the rest of the trip we got sago pudding every day, and they never did find where the raw sago was hidden.

Surprisingly, when you consider the way we were fed, the one commodity that was in short supply in every trawler I ever sailed in was tea. Probably the owners felt that when we were supping tea we weren't working, so by keeping us short they removed the temptation. In all the distant water boats the skippers carried tea, sugar, and tinned milk in the bond, and each watch bought enough to last them the trip, so we could always brew a pot of 'special' in the middle of a steaming watch, or when fishing if we had the time. Most skippers would tip in four or five tins of milk and a pound of tea to each watch, thereby becoming entitled to a pot of 'spec' whenever it was brewed. The tea the owners put aboard was unlike any tea I've seen in the caddy at home. Different to the fine-grained stuff that comes out of a Typhoo packet, it was black, coarse, dusty, and had splinters in it the size of match sticks. I've heard tell it was the sweepings from the floors of the blending rooms, and I can believe it. When brewed it stained the mugs nearly black, and almost took the enamel off your teeth, especially when it had been stewing on the hot stove top for half an hour. It was strictly rationed. The cook would brew up about 8p.m. before turning in, and leave out three mashings to last through the night. The general custom was to put each measure of tea in a cut down milk tin, then mix the sugar in with the tea. If you didn't take sugar - too bad. Most cooks left out one tin of milk, others, more benevolent would leave out a tin and a half. When on passage, the bridge watch would brew up fifteen minutes before it was time to change watches so that the watch going off and the watch coming on got a drink. The third pot was brewed about 0530, just before the cook turned out. When fishing, in most ships the 'black squad' took over the teamaking, and made the brew-ups to coincide with hauling time. We made our special whenever the work routine allowed us the few minutes it took to make and drink it. The trawl and the fish always came first.

In spite of it all, the trawler cooks were a grand bunch of men.

One cook who, after doing a trip on a trawler that had been stationed in West Africa while on Admiralty service, and only recently been returned to fishing, complained to her owner that the boat was infested with cockroaches, and required fumigating.

"Don't be silly, Man. You're only imagining it," the owner told him. When the trawler docked the next trip the cook again requested an interview with the gaffer. Facing the great man across a polished table almost the size of a football pitch, the cook explained :

"Its about those cockroaches, Sir," he said, and taking a large baking powder tin from the bag he was carrying, he removed the lid, and emptied the contents onto the table top. With the swarm of big, brown insects scurrying all over the table top trying to find a hiding place, he added, "Don't worry about them things, Sir. We are only imagining them."

Penned up all day in solitary confinement in the hell hole of a galley, their food insulted three times a day, and being able to draw on a string of obscenities potent enough to blister the paintwork on a tank, they reserved their verbal vemon to throw at the weather. The only time I heard a cook curse at a man was when, hammering into a gale in an attempt to catch a tide, a particularly violent roll threw a pan off the stove a few minutes before mealtime. Came the mild curse (for a trawler cook) "Why can't the stormy bastard up there ease this syphilitic cow in while we get dinner over."

The cook's domain. A trawler's galley.

Chapter Twelve

THINGS THAT COME UP
IN THE TRAWL

Seafaring in any type of ship in times of peace or war, carries with it an element of danger. All these dangers are compounded for the men that man the distant water trawlers.

On passage to and from the fishing grounds they are sailing far to the north of the regular trade routes, and when fishing they are remote from any organized rescue services, therefore in any emergency they must rely on their own resources, and the help of their own kind for most of the time. To put it bluntly, when they find themselves in the mire, they have to claw their own way out as best they can.

Often they are running off to shoot their gear, or battling through Atlantic storms, when vessels engaged in more sedate trades are hove to, or seeking shelter. On the fishing ground they have to handle heavy weights, and operate running wire gear on ice clad warping drums, in atrocious weather conditions, with the attendant risk to life and limb. They carry no doctor, and may be more than a hundred miles of storm swept seas away from the nearest medical assistance in the event of an accident.

When gutting the fish in the pounds on the foredeck the men are working close to the trawl warps. The trawl can come fast on an obstruction at any time, and when it does a tremendous strain is put on these three inch wires. If one of them parts, and this often happens, the parted ends backlash across the deck. If a crewman is hit, he will be severely injured at best, decapitated at worst.

Every trawlerman, regardless of where he is fishing, faces other hazards that are not applicable to the men that crew other types of vessel. The gear he tows along the seabed is not selective in what it catches. Besides cod and haddock, it will pick up big stones that may weigh well over a ton, and all sorts of other debris. Getting these unwelcome catches on board, especially in foul weather, requires skill and teamwork if some crewman is not to be dragged overboard. That mishap has occurred more than once.

Some of the objects the trawl catches can be lethal. Throughout the war, convoys bound for Russia sailed round Iceland, passed close to Bear Island, and crossed the Barents Sea on their way to Murmansk and Archangel. En route they were attacked by submarines, and bombed by aircraft. Not a pleasant run, the Russian convoys, and many Allied ships and German submarines were sunk, only to turn up as 'fasteners' after the war to foul the trawl gear.

Some of the bombs missed their target, failed to explode, and sank to the seabed. Not all the torpedoes found their way into the belly of the ship they had been aimed at, and when their motor stopped they sank to the bottom. Occasionally the firing mechanism in depth charges would be faulty, and fail to detonate the charge, or they would be washed off the deck in bad weather, and add to the pile. Thousands of mines were laid, and many broke away from their moorings, or were swept to the surface and sunk by gunfire by the minesweepers. All these instruments of war contained enough explosives to blow a much bigger ship than a trawler out of the water, and the older they get, the more unstable they become. They lie harmlessly on the bottom until brought to the surface in the fishermans net.

One Grimsby trawler working off the Norwegian coast exploded a mine on the bottom with her gear. The blast of the explosion, nearly half a mile astern, blew all the band irons off the iron bobbins, and when heaved up they looked like a string of shelled peas. Another trawler from the same port hit a floating mine while towing her gear. The resultant explosion blew off the forecastle and killed the watch below who were asleep at the time. What was left of the ship, and the remainder of the crew reached Tromso in safety.

A Hull trawler, the St. Hubert, dragged up a mysterious object in the net. It was heaved for'ard and lashed up secure. Three days after being brought on board it began to tick, exploded, and killed three of the crew. Despite the efforts of the remaining crew members, St. Hubert sank six hours later, the survivors being picked up by another Hull trawler. Turning over the records since the end of the 1914-18 Great War you'll find many such incidents, and

the above examples demonstrate just how deadly these rusting, obscene relics of war can be.

The official advice trawlermen are given is that when they pick up a mine in the trawl they should lower it back to the seabed, and tow it until the mine chafes its way out of the net. That is great when you know you have caught a mine. The trouble is, most times you don't. You drop the bobbins on board and the net, containing the mine and maybe a hundred baskets of fish, is leading off from the ship's side. The fish will float up in the top part of the belly of the trawl, and the heavy mine will work its way down to the codends where you can't see it. All you know is that you have something heavy in the net, and a big stone will behave in exactly the same way. When you heave the fish down to the codends they will cover whatever weight is at the bottom, hiding it from view, and until you have heaved the bag aboard, untied the codline, and emptied the codends, you won't know what you've caught. You pick up far, far more stones than mines, and the trawler skipper doesn't exist that would give up a hundred baskets of fish on the off chance that the weight in the codends might be something more deadly than a brick.

Once you have a mine on deck the advice offered is that you contact a coast station by radio, and a team of naval explosive experts will be dispatched to you to remove the detonator and render it harmless. That is fine if you are working in home waters where this assistance can be with you in a very short time, but if you are fishing in the remote regions of the Arctic its a different matter. The mine disposal squad could take days to reach you, and a gale could spring up any time. The last thing you want is a ton of dynamite, probably in an unstable condition, sitting on the foredeck, and the ship tossing about.

When a mine has been swept, and sunk by rifle fire, its case will be punctured. Lying on the seabed for years, water might have seeped through rusting seams. It is reasonable to assume that over the years the explosive charge might have become saturated with seawater. From the moment the mine lands on deck those explosives start to dry out. I'll want a lot of convincing that T.N.T. isn't more likely to explode when it is dry than when it is soaked with seawater. Therefore the accepted method of disposal was to steam to the nearest deep water, too deep for trawling, and get the obscenity over the side and back to the seabed, where it couldn't do any harm. And the quicker the better.

For the individual, picking up a mine didn't happen often, but there were a lot of mines on the seabed, and there were a lot of trawlers fishing, but generally, unless you were in the vicinity, you only heard about those occasions when there was an explosion and loss of life. Compare the risk factor with that of pedestrians trying to cross a busy road. Only a small proportion of them get run over. These are the ones we hear about. The near misses never make the headlines.

If you are mathematically minded you might like to try to quantify the probability of picking a mine up in the net. To do this, as no official statistics exist, I can only draw on my own experience. Excluding three or four occasions during the war when we were fishing too close to a minefield, and found

a mine, complete with mooring wire and sinker, hung on the gear, my tally consists of one land mine, a rusty relic of the 1914-18 War which had probably been part of a redundant stock of explosives dumped at sea for want of a cheaper method of disposal, one depth charge, and six mines. Taking a twenty five year period from 1945 till 1970, and assuming 150 days fishing a year, with an average of eight hauls a day we can take the approximate number of hauls to be: 25 X 150 X 8 = 30,000 hauls.

In those 30,000 hauls I caught an explosive gadget eight times, or once every 3,750 hauls, giving about 0.027 of 1 per cent. Not a very high risk factor, but a better chance than winning a fortune on the football pools, and some lucky punter does that every week.

One trip, while working on East Bank in the Barents Sea, we hauled the gear. After dropping the bobbins on board, we were horrified to see a mine hung up on the net in the top of the belly of the trawl. The weather was fine, no swell to speak of, and we were able to get a rope round the belly below the mine , preventing it from rolling down to the codends. We were then able to cut the net around the mine without it banging on the ship's side. As it sank back into the dark depths we breathed again. There wasn't much fish in the net, and as we pulled it aboard it was obvious that we had something heavy in the codends. This gave no cause for concern because every haul we had been catching a quantity of duff, a sponge-like organism that looks like a suet duff, grows to the size of a football or bigger, and weighs very heavy in the water. We heaved the codends aboard, and I made my way for'ard to untie the codline, while the rest of the lads started to repair the cut net. I'm not a brave man, and what I saw stopped my heart beating, and turned my guts to water. Visible through the mesh of the hanging bag was the rusting carcass of another mine. No bag was ever lowered to the deck more gently.

On another occasion, I was bosun with Skipper Barry Jacklin in the Thuringia, and fishing on Eldyer Bank, off the southwest Iceland coast. One haul we had a good catch of cod, big heavy fish, and decided to heave it aboard in one lift. The huge bag of fish, over three ton, swung inboard over the rail, and I released the codline. As the fish cascaded into the fish pounds there was a dull thud, the sound a big stone makes when it drops on the deck. Heaving the codends clear of the 'big stone' revealed the biggest mine I have ever seen. It stood almost shoulder high, and with a coat of grey paint, looked brand new.

"Is it a mooring buoy?" Barry called from the bridge window.

"No, I think its a magnetic mine," I yelled back.

We steamed off to the deep water and got rid of our deadly catch.

Later, Dave, the mate, who had been below at the time told me, "I hear you had some fun while I was turned in. The Old Man told me he laid down on his bathroom floor while you were dumping the mine over the side."

Next day I mentioned it to Barry. "Dave told me you went down to the bathroom while we were putting that mine over the side, Skipper," I said.

"Yes, John," he grinned, "Them things are dangerous, you know."

I didn't need telling that. "Don't worry," I said, "the size of that one, had it gone off there would have been a bit for everybody."

Another trip at Bear Island, we heaved the trawl up full of codling, enough to split into four or five lifts. When I let go the first bag, what I took to be an empty oil drum dropped out of the codends, and settled upside down, and three parts covered with fish, in the after end of the fish pound. I actually sat on it while tying the codline getting the rest of the fish aboard. It was two hours later, when we had nearly gutted the fish round it, that we discovered that the 'oil drum' was an unexploded depth charge.

Over the centuries, hundreds of ships and cargoes have been lost at sea, and there must be more treasures lying on the seabed than there is stowed away in Swiss bank vaults and London depositories. You would think that some of this booty would find its way into the fishermens' nets from time to time, but I've never been lucky. The only thing of value that I've ever trawled up is fish. I've caught anchors of all shapes and sizes, some black with age and crusted with barnacles, but more often the four pronged variety that long line fishermen use to peg out their lines. I've picked up huge sections of rusting ironwork, the tragic remains of some long-forgotten shipwreck, and parts of wartime aircraft that had failed to return to base. One haul off the south coast of Iceland we caught about thirty lengths of waterlogged timber, probably once the deck cargo of some unfortunate timber boat. They were about twenty feet long, with a twelve inch cross section, and it took about four hours to get them aboard, and repair the damage to the net.

One year a Spanish cargo boat carrying a deck cargo of Seville oranges that were probably destined for Ticklers jam factory in Grimsby, came to grief in a North Sea storm off the mouth of the Humber. I heard that when the weather abated the trawlers in the area had good catches of oranges. I don't know if they had any monetary value, but I've no doubt they made an addition to the men's diet.

I caught my strangest, and most unpleasant catch off the Murmansk coast; a dead horse. What a horse would be doing at sea, so far into the Arctic, I can't imagine. Swinging round on the bridles, with the trawl over a hundred yards away to windward, you could smell it. I've caught whale ribs and vertebra that have given off a faint, unpleasant odour, but I have never experienced the sickening smell that was wafting from the net on this occasion. Untying the codline, with my face inches from the bag, the overpowering stench of petrification made me vomit. After we had shot the gear we had to dispose of the stinking carcass. First we tried to heave it over the side. Holding our breath as best we could, we managed to get a becket round its middle, and attempted to heave it overboard with the Yo Yo. No joy. As soon as the weight came on the wire, the becket cut through the thing, and left us with two halves to play with. Finally, as a last resort, we unshipped all the deck boards, used the deck hose to swill the putrefied flesh away, and then shovelled the bones overboard. Despite frequent wash downs it clung to the ship and attacked our nostrils for days.

For me, and for most trawlermen, anything that came up in the trawl other than fish meant work rather than riches.

Note:

The explosion aboard the St. Hubert occurred on 29th August 1960. In addition to the three crewmen killed instantly, the skipper, G.H. Ness, was seriously injured. Despite his injuries, Skipper Ness strived to keep the badly damaged trawler afloat for six hours in a gale force wind. St. Hubert finally had to be abandoned, and she sank close in to Hornoy Light, Vardo. All her remaining crew members were picked up be the Hull trawler Prince Charles which had been standing by the stricken vessel, but sadly, Skipper Ness died of his injuries.

The Grimsby Trawler 'Notts County', Lost at Isafjord, North West Iceland in the violent storm of 4th February 1968 (see chapter 13).

Chapter Thirteen

BLACK ICE

If you are a regular visitor to the Arctic Seas during the winter months, sooner or later you will find yourself toiling in sub-zero temperatures so low that the coldness has to be experienced to be believed. Coldness so intense that before you have been on deck an hour there is an inch or more of ice on your sou'wester, and in the galley, ice forms on the steel plating not more than a couple of feet from the hot stove. Unbelievable, but true.

Conditions are not always like that. If they were, no amount of money would coax men to venture deep into these desolate, frozen regions in search of a crust. You get extreme conditions, and you get spells when things are not quite as bad. You might be very lucky and encounter an almost Indian summer. Not often, admittedly, but it has been known.

Temperatures below minus 50 degrees Centigrade are not uncommon, and although highly unpleasant, they do not stop the work. Apart from the risk of frostbite these low temperatures pose no danger to ship or crew. In my opinion, a view based on over thirty years experience voyaging to these waters, the coldest fishing grounds are those in the north and east parts of the Barents Sea, and the area around Bear Island.

To give rise to danger to the trawler the very low temperatures must be accompanied by severe gale or storm force winds, and very heavy seas. Conditions in which the wind-driven spray freezes to the masts, rigging, and superstructure. The weight of this ice accretion raises the trawler's centre of gravity, and if the build up of ice is allowed to continue, eventually the centre of gravity will become higher than the meta centre. Once this state is reached the ship will have unstable equilibrium, and the danger of capsizing is very real. The trawlermen are well aware of this danger, and naturally, they are well versed in the course of action to be taken if the danger is to be averted.

The distant water trawler is a robust creature, designed and built to withstand the battering dished out by the normal Arctic climatic conditions, and more. It is when the elements combine to produce degrees of violence that greatly exceed normality that tragedies occur. From time to time, freezing temperatures and storm force winds coincide. A trawler caught in these conditions is forced by the heavy seas to dodge head to wind, and the amount of heavy water being shipped prevents the crew from going on deck to chop the away the ice accruing on the top parts. As the weight of ice builds up, the trawler starts to heel over. Unless the weather moderates she will soon reach the point of no return and capsize. The conditions that give rise to the foundering are such that no ship can live in them, and so prevent any effective rescue operation. The crew of the stricken ship are doomed. Within minutes of entering the water their blood will have frozen in their veins. Such is the price of fish.

Earlier I expressed the opinion that the coldest fishing grounds I have worked are those in the Barents Sea and around Bear Island, yet I have never experienced the peril of capsizing through ice accretion in those waters. I'll go further than that. I have never heard tell of any trawler lost in those areas for that reason. Dire peril only threatens the trawler when storm force winds and freezing temperatures occur together. At Bear Island the severe gales occur with the wind from the southwest. This sou'west wind, often topping forty or fifty knots, is relatively warm, and tends to blow the frost away. Further east in the Barents Sea, the cold wind is the one that blows from the southeast. Super chilled while crossing the frozen wastes of Siberia, it hits you like the draught from a blast freezer. Intensely cold it may be, but it rarely gusts above force eight. The tidal streams in the Barents Sea tend to be weak, consequently the seas generated don't prevent the work of clearing the ice formation away.

If you check the records over the last fifty years, you will find that all the trawlers lost through icing up came to grief off the north or nor'west coast of Iceland. At the risk of being shot at, I suggest that whenever a catastrophe of that nature occurred, somewhere along the line, either a skipper had made an error of judgement, or a watchkeeper had delayed too long before calling the 'Old Man' out. The underlying cause of that error may have been

overtiredness, inexperience of the conditions that can prevail in the area or the speed that conditions can change, or the pressure exerted by financial considerations. Or maybe a combination of all those factors.

It may be that a trawler is enjoying good fishing when a gale of wind makes it necessary to pull the gear aboard. In order to be on the spot when the weather moderates, thus losing no time, the skipper decides to remain on the ground and, hove to, ride out the storm. This is normal practice. Only on this occasion the wind changes direction and increases in violence, and with the change of wind the temperature drops dramatically. Shelter, in the form of one of the fjords, may be only thirty or forty miles away, but by now the sea is so heavy that the trawler, its stability already reduced by ice accretion, has no alternative other than to keep head to wind if she is to remain afloat. All round the clock, her crew will be on deck chopping ice off her, and if the weather deteriorates no further, or if the duration of the storm is not too long, she will survive, and the gamble will have paid off.

But sometimes the weather doesn't moderate. It gets worse, and the temperature drops further. Ice builds up faster than the exhausted, half-frozen men can chop it away. With the increasing height of the seas, the trawler, pitching and rolling her guts out, starts to ship heavy water, making it impossible for the men to work on deck any longer. The deadly load of ice builds up unchecked, and the end of the drama is not far away.

If the weight of ice hasn't brought the wireless aerials down the doomed trawler will be in contact with those ships that had ran for shelter while there was still time. She will also put out a Mayday call which the Icelandic coastguard and the gunboats will acknowledge, but this is only a token gesture. The skipper knows full well that no ship afloat could battle through the prevailing weather conditions to render him assistance, and even if they could get to him, by the time they arrived they would be in the same desperate trouble that he was in. Some of the trawlers, and one of the Icelandic gunboats will leave the fjords to make the futile attempt at rescue, but before covering ten miles of the distance, they too will be iced up to a degree that forces them to give up. As the stricken ship heels further over, her exhausted crew resign themselves to their fate. Over the radio they may relay last messages to their loved ones ashore. Then, suddenly, communications cease.

A day or two later, when the wind has died down a little, the ships will search the area. They won't find anything; they never do. Maybe a week later, a hundred miles away, some ship will pick up an empty life raft, the sole remains of a fine ship, and her twenty man crew.

It doesn't always end like that. For every trawler that has been lost, over the years there must have been scores of near misses. Ships encased in icy coffins, that by a combination of superlative seamanship, inimitable feats of physical endeavor, a giant slice of luck, and the grace of God, have clawed their way out of the icy hell and reached the comparative safety of one of the fjords. Pay a visit to one of the taverns in the vicinity of the fish docks in Hull or Grimsby, and get chatting to some of the veteran

deep water trawlermen. Men who have spent year after year trawling along the 'Hindenburg Line', Stranda Flat, and the deep water nor'west of North Cape prior to the imposition of the 200 mile fishing limits. Get a few pints of ale down them, and when they are sufficiently inebriated you may be able to steer the conversation round to the Icelandic winters, and persuade them to recount details of personal experiences when their lives hung on a slender thread, and somehow, for one reason or another, the angry seas rejected them, and mercifully, they lived to fish again. In that respect, I am no different to those men. I have had my share of thrills, spills, and frights, but on only one occasion have I had serious misgivings that maybe I had reached the end of the road, that perhaps this time the ship, good as she was, wouldn't pull through. That we were enacting the last throw of the dice.

The Thuringia was a good ship. As sea-kindly as any you were likely to meet. Built at Beverley by Cook, Welton and Gemmel in 1944 for the Admiralty, she was one of the Military Class. 178 feet long, 30 feet beam, and nearly 600 tons gross, she was released for fishing at the end of the war. I signed on her as bosun when Northern Trawlers gobbled up the Butt Group in the sixties, and she became my home for the greater part of the next two years, fishing in Icelandic waters the whole time. For the first twelve months I served under the late Skipper George Lill, and for the remainder of the time with Skipper Barry Jacklin. This is the story of the last trip under George's command. A trip during which Thuringia, good sea boat that she was, was almost overwhelmed. A trip when twenty men stared death in the face, and somehow, by incredible good fortune, managed to claw their way to safety. It is a story very little different from the many you can hear in the bars along Hessle Road or Freeman Street.

The start of the trip was no different to that of dozens of previous trips. Dave, the mate, and I shared a taxi, arriving on the North Wall at about 0430 on a miserable, wet, windy winter morning, trying to throw off the effects of the night's revelry we'd enjoyed at the Beachcomber Club. The muffled figure of Bill Batty, the runner, was stood among the puddles on the quayside, trying in vain to keep the driving rain off the already sodden crew list. Seeing Dave and I emerge from the taxi, he crossed our names of the list, and called out the odds like a parson preaching the last rites. "Only the cook to come."

As Dave and I were the only souls within earshot, the call could only be interpreted as an admonition that he expected the mate and bosun to be aboard earlier, so the ship could get the hell to sea and he could get home and to bed for a couple of hours. Or maybe he was repeating the drill from force of habit. Either way, we didn't take much notice.

Aboard the ship things were normal. Most of the deck crowd were grouped in the galley supping tea, and looking the worse for wear. "Want a dram, John?", one of the lads asked, brandishing a bottle with about three inches of rum in it.

"Later, when we get clear," I replied. "Are all the lifelines rigged?"

"All done. The watchman has rigged them and stowed all the loose gear," one of them chipped in.

I had just time to descend the companionway and stow my seabag when the engineroom telegraph jangled. I heard the mate bark, "Stand by, men," as I made my way up to the bridge. Ten minutes later, as the men for'ard stowed the mooring ropes under the whaleback, and scurried down the fo'c'sle out of the blustering wind and rain, Thuringia glided through the 45 foot lock and headed into the Humber.

The passage to Iceland was accomplished without incident, the weather no better, no worse, than you might expect in January.

George Lill was a very experienced skipper. In his middle fifties, he had been trawling all his working life, except for a break in the war years when he had commanded a minesweeper. Although he had a wealth of experience to draw on, most of the time he had worked the Norwegian coast and Barents Sea grounds, hence when compared with the specialists, his all round knowledge of Iceland was probably sketchy. Throughout the previous year we had worked the comparatively milder south and east coasts, never venturing west of the Westman Isles, nor north or west of Langanes. We never ploughed up any trees, but we always caught enough fish to ensure we wouldn't starve.

Initially, this trip followed the same pattern as all the others. We kicked off at the 'Whaleback' and progressively worked our way along the east coast, trying our luck at Vopna, Seydisfiord, the Telegraph pitch, and finally ending up at Langanes. For the time of the year the weather had been kind, chilly rather than freezing, and just enough wind to keep the gear off the side when hauling. But fish were scarce, our best haul being about thirty baskets, and after a week's work we had only about 800 kits down the fishroom.

All the Company's ships fishing at Iceland were working in the North Cape area, and according to the reports we were getting on the twice daily schedule, some of them were catching very good hauls. Eventually, after a very depressing haul, and two days persuasion from Dave, who financed an expensive wife, and myself, who had just taken possession of a new bungalow and a big mortgage, George decided to pull the gear aboard and head, full speed, for the reported bonanza. That decision was error number one, although at the time, in view of the fishing reports, and the size of the trips going home from the Cape, it seemed the sensible course of action at the time. The eighteen hour hike along the north side was pleasant enough. After rounding the finger-like peninsula of Langanes the snow fell continuously, the flakes as big as postage stamps, but there was hardly a breath of wind. The only event on our westward passage worth mentioning was having to put the helm hard over to avoid a large 'growler', nearly as big as a bungalow, which loomed out of the snow ahead. The big iceberg that had probably calved it had been blipping on the radar screen for half an hour as we approached, so the presence of ice was not unexpected, and we were keeping a careful lookout.

We arrived on the fishing ground nor'west of North Cape only to find the dozen or so ships there spread out over a wide area. Not a good sign. When there is fish about the trawlers tend to group to-gether, or appear in a line, all trying to be in the same depth of water where the fish is. Chatting to one of his pals on the V.H.F., George learned that what fish there had been had took off days ago. As so often happened, we had come chasing after 'wireless fish'; that is, fish that had been caught days before it had appeared on the fishing reports.

We had three blank hauls, then the weather broke. The freshening sou'west wind quickly increased to gale force, whipping up seas like mountains. We scrambled the gear aboard, lashed it up secure, and hove to wind and sea for the next twelve hours. Those ships nearing the end of their time left for home, the others scattered. With no sign of moderation in the weather, and with the weather forecasts equally gloomy, the skipper decided to return to the east side of Iceland.

Taking the steaming time involved into account, we had only three days fishing time left, and that fact led up to error number two. We took the shorter passage along the north coast instead of the longer route down the west and south coasts. The stage was all set for error number three; an error that dropped us in the shit up to our necks.

We set off on the two hundred mile steam, an easterly course with wind and sea on the starboard quarter. George took the bridge watch until midnight. He had been on the bridge nearly twenty-four hours when he handed over the watch and retired for a long overdue sleep. The relieving watchkeeper, though uncertificated, was a very experienced seaman. Shortly after midnight the wind veered to the nor'west, and it started to freeze. The 'Old Man' should have been called out, but contrary to standing orders, he wasn't. That was error number three, and it was a mistake that nearly sealed the fate of Thuringia and her twenty man crew.

I was called out to go on watch at 0630. Sat on my seat locker, pulling on my gear, I could sense something was wrong. When you have sailed in a ship for any length of time you get to know its motion in a seaway, and your muscles automatically tense to compensate for that motion. Thuringia's movement seemed far too sluggish, her roll was too slow, and the pause in the heeled position before she returned to the vertical was too long.

As soon as I stepped out on to the deck to make my way to the bridge the reason was apparent. I have never, before or since, seen as great a weight of ice be allowed to accumulate on a ship. The lifeboats and davits were unrecognizable as such, just solid blocks of ice. The engine room ventilators were encased in a cocoon of ice from base to cowl at least a foot thick, and looking up to the top of the wheelhouse, I could see the radar towers standing like pillars of salt above the white wall that had formed between the handrails. I could hardly squeeze along the veranda to get into the bridge on account of the ice formation on the rails one side, and the side of the chartroom the other.

Entering the wheelhouse, I ignored the "Good morning, John" and took stock. Apart from the small circle of revolving glass at the centre of the Kent Clearview, the windows were all iced up. Peering through the Clearview I could see that the fore end of the ship was little different to the after end. The ice had built up on the whaleback to a thickness almost as high as the handrails, the centre part

raised a couple of feet where it covered the windlass. The fore stays, the bottom ends of the shrouds, and the gallows support bars were coated with ice at least a foot thick. From the houndsband, the iron band half way up the foremast, to which the blocks and the top ends of the shrouds were shackled, the ice had crept downward, forming a triangular arch joining port and starboard rigging, and upwards almost to the navigation lights. Altogether there must have been forty or fifty tons of the stuff. We should have started chopping it away hours ago.

"Why didn't you call the Old Man when it started to freeze?" I asked.

"At first I thought it was just soft snow," the watchkeeper replied lamely, "then, as it was nearly watch time I thought it best to wait till you came up. We passed Grimsey three hours ago, ten miles off. The radar packed up an hour ago." Telling the man why the radar had packed up, and commenting on his criminal negligence, or inane ignorance, would have been pointless at that moment. That would come later. Right now it was imperative that we started chopping, and the sooner we started the better.

"You'd better call all hands," I said, "I'll call the Old Man."

When George arrived on the bridge and saw the state of his ship he wasn't very happy. After one minute of recriminations, "I'll let her lay. Put a couple of men on the bridge top, and take the rest for'ard and try to clear the mast and rigging. Concentrate on getting the top ice down if you can," he ordered.

We started to clear the ice about 0700. We had

no hot water hose. The pipelines had frozen solid hours ago, and would have taken hours to clear. And time was one commodity we didn't have. Armed with an assortment of fire axes, choppers, spanners, and crowbars, twelve men set to work.

Laid broadside to the freezing nor'west wind, Thuringia rolled sluggishly in the heavy, white-capped rollers. First we knocked the ice off the lifelines. Then two men started the dangerous job of clearing the fore stays. The ice on the deck of the whaleback was nearly as high as the top of the rails, so one slip and they would have been over the side. First they had to clear the fore ends of the rail, then secure themselves with a line to the cleared end. Only then could they attack the ice on the stays. First chopping off the ice at the bottom to as high as they could reach, then hammering the cleared wire until the vibration caused the tube of ice to slide down to them. Meantime, the mate and I started on the rigging. "Race you to the top, John," he called.

"You're on," I called back, "the last to the top shows the boys his cock," with far more humour than I felt.

Before we had been chopping half an hour we were sweating like pigs, and except for a couple of five minute breaks when the galley boy, wrapped up like Father Christmas, brought a jug of hot coffee, we continued working until dinner time. By then you could see where we'd been. The stays were clear, and we had worked three parts up the rigging. We were gaining ground, but with daylight the wind had started to increase, and was howling through the rigging like a banshee. With sweating bodies, fingers and toes numb with cold, and faces cut and bleeding from flying ice splinters, we trooped off the deck for our meal.

Half an hour later we were back on deck. The wind was really piping now, and the white-crested seas were rolling out of the curtain of hail like mountains. During the time we had been at dinner an inch or so of ice had formed on the cleared ratlines, and as I knocked it away to ensure a safe foothold, a huge sea, a giant among giants, roared down on us. I heard the mate's roar "WATER" above the howl of the wind, and wrapped myself round the middle shroud. Thuringia tried hard, God bless her, and normally she would have rode the sea like a cork, and shook the water off her deck like a spaniel shakes off water when it climbs out of a river. But now she was handicapped by the insidious weight of ice she was carrying aloft. As the mountain of water roared down on her, she leaned slowly to meet it, rose up as it passed underneath her, and as it passed she heeled over to leeward. Clinging to the rigging, half blinded by spray, I could only watch, petrified, as water poured over the lee rail. With the weight of water pouring aboard Thuringia continued to lay over.

"Jesus Christ", I thought, "she's going." But Thuringia didn't capsize. She stayed heeled over at a crazy angle, almost on her beam ends, her starboard rail submerged, side lights nearly in the water, and the sea surging across the foredeck as far as the hatch coamings. She was heeled so far over that the Yo Yo derrick seemed parallel with the surface of the sea, and I had the inane notion that if a seagull had perched on the derrick head, the extra weight would have been sufficient to have turned us over.

But there weren't any seagulls about. They had more sense than us, and had long since sought refuge under the land. Looking for'ard, I saw the top half of the mate's distinctive yellow oilskins above the water, as he tried to haul one of the deckies to safety under the whaleback, that is if any place aboard the ship could be called safe. In one hell of a hurry, I pulled myself along the lifeline, scaled the casing, and entered the wheelhouse.

Water had squeezed through the sides of the door on the low side, and washing around the hot pipes, had filled the place with steam. Through the chartroom door I could see the Old Man heaped in a bundle on the deck. When the ship had heeled over he had probably been thrown across the room, striking his head on the bulkhead. First aid would have to wait. If the ship couldn't be brought back on an even keel, all the first aid in the world wouldn't help. My actions were instinctive. If the Admiralty Manual of Seamanship contains any advice on how to handle a ship top heavy with ice, carrying a sixty degree list, and wallowing in a force ten gale, I've never come across it. I rang the telegraph Full Ahead and put the helm hard over to port, the high side. The telegraph was answered immediately. The chief must have been standing by the stop valve, wondering what the hell was going on. An age passed and I felt the vibration as the engine revolutions built up. Another age passed and the rudder began to grip. Slowly, very slowly, the compass card began to revolve as the ship's head turned into the wind. As she turned, she struggled upright. The old lass wasn't going to throw the towel in yet. As the ship settled on an even keel, I dropped the engine

revs, and eased the helm. The tension flowed out of me, I said a silent prayer for the men that had built such a fine sea boat, then I shit myself. It had been a near thing, and I guess I'm not made of the stuff heroes are made of.

That wasn't the end of the ordeal, it was only the beginning.

We kept head to wind for the rest of the afternoon. If anything, the wind, still from the northwest, blew harder, and it was still freezing hard. The heavy water we were shipping over the fo'c'sle head rendered work fore side the superstructure impossible so we set about clearing the ice off the after end. By teatime, at 1800 hours, we had knocked off all the ice on the ventilators, boat davits, after mast, and the after end of the wheelhouse. All the double bottom tanks were pressed up to eliminate free surface effect, and lower the centre of gravity as far as possible. Now, all we could do was wait, keep the after end clear of ice, and pray for a moderation in the weather. By now, all the ice we had cleared off the fore end had been replaced with a fresh coating of the stuff, and we were in serious trouble.

There was only two places of refuge we could consider trying to get to, both about forty miles distant. To reach Grimsey Isle the wind would be three or four points on the starboard bow, and that option could be ruled out. Steaming hard enough to make any headway in the prevailing conditions would result in so much spray coming aboard that the ice accretion would capsize the ship before we had covered half the distance. That only left the shelter afforded by the Langanes peninsula. To reach there the wind would be on the starboard quarter, and although we would generate far less spray than when steaming into the wind, there would be the danger of pooping, that is, shipping heavy water over the stern, with the attendant risk of running the ship under.

The skipper had recovered somewhat from the knock on the head, and after tea decided to try and run for Langanes. Before we had been down wind ten minutes, a sea piled over the stern, filling the fore deck with water as high as the tops of the gallows, scaring the pants off the bridge watch, and forcing him to heave to. We had tried all the options. Now we could only wait and hope. As I came in off the deck after a spell chopping, the galley boy poured me out a mug of tea. A young lad, scarcely sixteen, looking very lonely, and very frightened. "Are we going to be alright, Bosun?" he asked. "'Course we are, Kid," I said with an enforced grin, and a confidence I didn't feel, "this time next week you'll be telling your pals all about it." He seemed reassured. How do you tell a youngster, hardly out of short pants, that he might be dead before breakfast time. If trawlermen have guardian angels, ours worked overtime that night. The first miracle occurred about two hours before the skipper was due to go off watch at midnight. I was sat on the seat locker in my cabin, skimming through the pages of a girlie magazine. Tired as we all were, only an idiot would have been able to sleep through the peril we were in. Each time the ship rolled, men held their breath until she returned to the vertical. Suddenly there was a loud crash, and Thuringia shuddered as if hit by a giant sledge hammer. Her stern reared out of the water, lifting me off the locker, the engines raced in protest, the lights flickered, went out, and came on again.

"What the fucking hell now," I heard the mate curse from his cabin across the alleyway. "Get your gear on, Kiddo," I called back, reaching for my seaboots, "he'll want us before long."

I had hardly got the words out when we heard the clump of boots on the ladder.

Rigged, we turned to on deck. The storm was at its height, the wind howled and screamed at us, and the hail stung our faces. In the light of the floodlights the foredeck looked like a bomb had exploded on it. A wall of water, probably hundreds of tons of it, had hit the ship head on. All the wooden deck boards had been smashed and carried away. The heavy iron gratings were strewn about the deck, bent into S and U shapes by the force of the water as it crashed aboard. The wireless aerials had been brought down, and the deck lights on the mast had been torn away, one of the lights still swilling to and fro across the duck pond, its severed cable trailing behind it. Two pair of fifty fathom three inch wire cables that had been coiled and lashed to the whaleback ladder were no longer there, and the fo'c'sle stove chimney had gone. The fish washing machine was heaped on top of the trawl winch, the bottle screws which held it to the tramlines having snapped like cotton, and the codends, which had been lashed to the handrail on the bollard with the codline, were stretched aft, the codline still hitched to the broken handrail. For'ard of the mast, and stretching under the whaleback, was a heap of chunks of ice, some as big as beer barrels. It took about fifteen minutes to square up the foredeck, hammer a plug into the stub of the stove chimney, and make everything that was left secure, then, half froze and wet through, we trooped off the deck.

That mountain of water which had theatened to overwhelm us, terrifying though it must have been for the men in the wheelhouse, was our salvation, because in the few seconds when it crashed over us it brought down all the top icing, a job it would have taken us hours to do, that is if we could have got at it, and in bringing down all that top weight, it restored some of the stability to the beleaguered ship.

With the top ice brought down and the consequent improvement in stability, perhaps we should have tried to make the passage to Langanes, but we didn't. Dave took the bridge watch from midnight and weatherwise it was probably the most demanding watch of the trip. Trying to doze on my seat locker, I was continually disturbed by the crash of water coming aboard.

I relieved the mate on the bridge at 0630 the next morning.

"No change in the weather, John," he said, "and he's left no orders. She's icing up again, so call the lads out if it moderates enough for us to get for'ard." With that, bleary eyed, he clumped off for breakfast.

Shortly after that the second miracle occurred.

As the bridge door slammed on the departing mate, I jammed myself in the wing of the bridge in front of the Clearview, one hip pressed against the steam radiator, the other resting on the telegraph. With the ship's head held to wind and sea, engine revolutions just sufficient to give steerage way, I stared through the revolving circle of glass at the angry white topped rollers that roared down, each one threatening to engulf us. As each one approached, Thuringia somehow managed to lift her head to meet it. As each sea thundered past, her head went down, spray lashed the front of the bridge adding another coat to the accretion of ice, and water surged over the breakwater on the fo'c'sle head, cascaded down onto the foredeck, swilled about among the slush ice, and finally drained away through the after scuppers as the ship's head lifted to meet the next sea.

I had been on watch about an hour, dawn was just breaking, when I detected, sensed rather than saw, a slight change in the fury of the elements. The wind hadn't changed. It was still howling and screaming, but the sea seemed to be just a little less violent. Batches of spray were still hammering the front of the bridge, but I realized that it was ten minutes since the last heap of heavy water had crashed over the stem. Pulling up the hood of my duffle coat and donning mittens, I left the comparative warmth of the wheelhouse to stand on the frozen veranda. With the wind tearing at the flaps of my coat, and face numbed by the intense cold, I studied the surface of the surrounding sea for a full fifteen minutes. Satisfied, I returned to the warmth of the wheelhouse, and brushed off the powdered ice which had formed on my coat. For a reason I wasn't to discover till late that night, the seas were moderating. Although the wind was still blowing as hard as it had ever done, the leading edges of the rollers were far less steep than they had been, and the white horses were fewer in number, and more widely scattered.

"Is it fining away, John? She seems to be steering better," the helmsman asked hopefully.

"I think so. Keep your fingers crossed," I told him, and made my way to the skipper's cabin to report.

George was hunched on his seat locker, elbows on the table, wrapped in a blanket. Hollow eyed from lack of sleep, he looked like two penny-worth of death warmed up. Two days without sleep, the knock on the head, combined with the mental stress he was under, wasn't doing him much good. Flesh and blood can only stand so much, and I believe the skipper was getting very close to breaking point, physically and mentally.

I've read a lot in the press lately about executive stress. True, a top executive might make a mistake that could lose his company business, might even bankrupt his company, and he might work very long hours. But when compared with the stress the trawler skipper is subjected to, I suggest that the polished executive, and the medic that attends him, don't know the meaning of the word. He won't be expected to work a twenty-four hour day, and he doesn't carry the burden of knowing that if he makes an error he, and all the people working under him, will perish. Our skipper had been subjected to that pressure for the last three days, and maybe it was beginning to show.

"The wind is still the same, but the swell seems to be moderating, skipper. I think she will run now," I told him.

"That's the nicest thing I've heard for a while," he replied quietly, "If you think she'll run put her straight down wind, then if she goes O.K., let her drop off a couple of points and head for Langanes. Use your discretion, John."

I returned to the wheelhouse. If anything, the sea looked a bit less hostile. "Nip down for some tea," I told the lookout, "and tell the cook and engineers I'll be bringing her round in fifteen minutes. The tea duly arrived, and I turned the ship about. At slow speed, she sailed down wind like a little duck. One hour later, after increasing engine revs twenty at a time, we were steaming full speed with the wind on the starboard quarter, and she never shipped more than a bucket full of water. A further two hours and I could just make out the long finger of land that was Langanes on the starboard bow. I don't think I've ever been as glad to see land. Another hour passed and we rounded the headland. I rang down 'Stop Engines' in smooth water, half a mile off the cliffs of Langanes peninsular. Our ordeal was all but over.

Lunch that day was a relaxed affair. Thuringia had sailed close to the pearly gates, and they all knew it. The tension eased out of them in a flow of raucous conversation. Later, when the necessary deck work was done there would be a lot of soiled underpants to wash, mine included.

After the meal Dave produced a bottle of Four Bells he had been hoarding and dished out a dram. Out of earshot of the rest of the lads he confided, "I didn't think we were going to get out of that lot, John."

"You weren't on your own, Laddie," I replied, "Leave the cards and horses alone this time in dock. We've used up this year's allocation of luck."

Then we set about the deck work. It was colder

than the inside of a butcher's cold room, but under the lee of the land, and in still water, the ship wasn't being thrown about like a bucking bronco, and we weren't being constantly drenched with icy water. After what we had been through, and with the threat of immediate peril no longer hanging over us, it was easy. The essential tasks were to clear the ice off the foremast and rigging, rig up the wireless aerials thus restoring contact with the outside world, and to clear the ice off the radar scanners and get the radar operational. On the passage south the weather conditions dictated that until we left Icelandic waters we would be steaming close in along a treacherous, rocky coast. Heavy snow falls and blizzards were the norm. The radar screen substituted for eyes. We would be blind without it.

With the wireless aerials rigged, the first ship we spoke to was the Icelandic gunboat Thor, and from him we learned why, though there had been no reduction in wind force, the sea had moderated sufficiently to allow us to reach safety. The constant northwest storm force winds had brought the sea ice down. The area where we had been dodging only a few hours previously was now an extensive ice field. Without radar, we had been unaware of the approaching ice, but the giant flows had formed a wind break, deadening the seas, thus allowing us to reach the land. It seems ironic that the very ice that nearly brought about our destruction threw us a lifeline.

There is not much more to tell. We never shot the gear again that trip, and after a brief stop at Thorshaven, in the Faroes, to get the funnel repaired, we proceeded to Grimsby. We landed 850 kits of fish which realized £6,500 at the auction. My share was about £90 before stoppages, for the three weeks work.

George never went to sea again after that trip. He swallowed the anchor, and found a job teaching at the fishing school. I can't say I blame him. Dave still had his expensive wife to support, and I still had a mortgage to pay off. Three days after landing the fish we were driving the Thuringia back to Iceland to challenge the Arctic again. Most of the crew came back with us.

That trip had a happy ending. Some ships weren't so fortunate.

During the fourth quarter of January 1955 a group of trawlers from Hull and Grimsby were fishing about fifty miles northwest of North Cape, Iceland. Lorella and Roderigo, both from Hull, were among them. Both were well found ships.

Lorella, 559 tons and 170 feet long, was built at Beverley in 1947. She was commanded by Skipper Steve Blackshaw, a veteran trawlerman who qualified for his skippers ticket in 1932. His vast experience on the Arctic fishing grounds had taught him all that had been written about seamanship, and quite a lot that hadn't.

Roderigo, formerly the Princess Elizabeth, also Beverley-built in 1950, was commanded by Skipper George Coverdale, forty years of age, and another very experienced fisherman, having held a skippers ticket for ten years.

As I recall it, the fishing had been very good, big bags of cod with a picking of haddock. Then it started to blow from the southwest. The area the ships were working, part of the Denmark Strait, is positioned in the angle formed by the east coast of Greenland to the west and the Polar ice cap to the north, and is as turbulent a stretch of water as any you will find on the planet. When the wind gets up, a calm sea transforms into a seething cauldron of white-crested mountains of water with a rapidity that has to be experienced to be appreciated. Another climatic characteristic of the region is the speed that the sou'west wind builds up to severe gale or storm force, then veers to the nor'west, bringing freezing conditions, and the resultant ice accretion. This is precisely what happened on the morning of the 25th January.

Most of the trawlers scrambled the gear aboard and dashed for shelter in Isafiord. Lorella and Roderigo decided to stay on the ground and weather out the coming storm, a decision that has often proved to be a winner. Only this time it led to a catastrophe. Later in the day, as conditions deteriorated at an alarming rate, Roderigo set off for shelter, but a distress call from another Hull trawler, the Kingston Garner I think, if memory serves me correct, diverted her. Arriving at the position given in the distress call Roderigo found nothing. The Kingston boat has reached safety, but had been unable to cancel the distress call.

By now Lorella was in desperate trouble, listing heavily and in mountainous seas. George Hobson, her wireless operator, put out a distress call. "We are on our side. Immediate assistance required." Roderigo answered the call. Maybe at that point in time Skipper Blackshaw could have saved himself and his ship, but a comrade needed help, and true to the tradition of his calling, he tried to render that

assistance. He actually got to Lorella, but by then, heavily iced up, Roderigo was in the same desperate plight as her sister. The men on the ships that had made the shelter of the land were glued to the radio as the drama unfolded.

"We are overturning," the Mayday crackled over the air, and Roderigo's wireless operator, George Leadly, continued to send out the call for seven minutes. "Conditions are too terrible to abandon ship. We require immediate assistance." Then silence.

All the bigger trawlers battled out of the comparative safety of the fjords to make the attempt at rescue, but by now the wind had reached hurricane force, and in impossible weather conditions they were forced to abandon the attempt, or suffer the same fate.

At least one trawler, the Lancella, refused to give up. In 75 knot winds, freezing temperatures, mountainous seas, and violent snow and hail squalls, she continued to search for the stricken vessels until the morning of the 27th January. The courage of these men was in vain. On 26th January 1955 the Lorella and Roderigo sank in those icy waters. Forty men perished and thirty children were rendered fatherless.

But the hungry sea still wasn't satisfied. That same day, close inshore, the 650 ton Icelandic trawler Egill Raudi sent out a distress call. She was capsizing off Ritur Huk. A shore party, with the help of another trawler, rescued 26 of her 34 man crew, the other eight men being lost. The survivors were clinging to the top of the bridge and the rigging, the only parts of the ship that remained above water. On 2nd February an Icelandic trawler picked up an empty liferaft 55 miles nor'west of the Cape that belonged to Roderigo. No other trace of the ill-fated ships was ever found.

The City of Hull is steeped in maritime tradition, and its womenfolk are well versed in the practice of mourning the loss of their men the sea has claimed. Many a tear has been shed on the end of Corporation Pier as wet eyes stared down the Humber, anxiously awaiting a husband, father, son or lover who would never return, and many times, women have gathered outside the offices of the trawler companies, frantic for news of some overdue ship. It was part of the life of a fisherman's family.

If ever you visit the city, have a look round the fishing section of the Docks Museum in the city centre. You won't be disappointed. Records held there show that as far back as the early 17th century boats from Hull were voyaging to the ice infested waters of Bear Island and Spitsbergen hunting whales, and in any one season, if half the men returned, it was considered a good year.

In modern times the first few weeks of 1968 were a time of misery. In a period of twenty-five days the sea claimed no less than sixty men, almost all of them from Hull. The first shock came on 11th January. The Hull trawler St. Romanus failed to report and was posted missing. Her last reported position was 110 miles nor'nor'east of Spurn Point, outward bound. Why she sank remains a mystery, no trace of her was ever found. So far south it is extremely unlikely that icing up played a part in the loss. The weather in the area was very bad at the time, and the general consensus of opinion was that she was overwhelmed by a freak sea. On the 26th January, 13 years to the day after the loss of Lorella and Roderigo, the Kingston Peridot iced up and sank with all hands on Skagagrunn, off the north coast of Iceland. The last contact with her was a radio conversation with another trawler, when her skipper said he was going to lay for a couple of hours while they chopped off some of the ice.

The flags were still fluttering at half mast on the poles around St. Andrew's Dock as Hull mourned the loss of forty of her sons when tragedy again hit the grief-stricken community. The heartbreaking news arrived that the Ross Cleveland (formerly Cape Cleveland) had foundered with the loss of eighteen of her nineteen men crew on the 4th February. Shortly after the Cleveland sank, the Grimsby trawler Notts County was driven ashore. Mercifully, thanks entirely to an incredible display of seamanship and courage by the crew of the Icelandic gunboat Odinn, eighteen men were snatched to safety. One man died of cold and exposure. Those two ships weren't the only casualties that wild night. A Fleetwood ship moored alongside the quay in Dyrafiord was torn from its moorings and driven ashore on the other side of the harbour, fortunately without loss of life, and there were scores of comparatively minor incidents, and hair-raising escapes. I'll describe the events of that day as viewed from the bridge of a trawler sheltering in Isafiord.

Maybe once in a decade or two the elements combine to produce conditions of unprecedented fury. On February 4th 1968 such conditions prevailed along the northwest coast of Iceland. It had been freezing hard for days before the wind came. We had been trawling along the south side of Isafiord Gully, and when the weather broke we were only about fourteen miles off West Head, the promontory that forms the starboard side of the entrance to Isafiord. Consequently, we were one of the first ships to reach shelter. Steaming in towards the land the black frost was so dense it blotted out the foremast, and without radar we would have been blind. At first we sheltered under the cliffs of Ritur Huk, dodging back under the land each time the wind drove us off into the choppy water in the middle of the fiord. Other ships arrived, throwing spray, and with their coating of ice looking like decorations on a Christmas cake.

The wind increased steadily throughout the morning, and eventually the height of the swell forced us to retreat further up the fiord. At its head, Isafiord divides. The starboard arm leads to the village and port facilities, the port arm, Jokulfjord, nicknamed 'Sleepy Valley' by the fishermen, forms a long narrow strip of deep water hemmed in by high cliffs. We spent the next hours hove to in Sleepy Valley. By now the wind speed had increased to a pitch I had never experienced before even in this wild region. Even at the head of the fiord, the ships had to go full ahead on the engines to maintain steerage. The air was so cold it was difficult to breathe. At the top end of Sleepy Valley I witnessed an example of survival technique I had never seen before. A large flock of eider ducks were flying under the cliffs, and settling on the water. They then climbed on each others backs, forming a huge ball. When the wind-driven ball of drifting ducks reached the chop-pier water in the middle of the fiord, they broke up, flew back under the cliffs, and repeated the manoeuvre.

Just how hard the wind blew that day is impossible to estimate. On wind gauges that register wind speeds up to 150 knots the pointer was going off the dial in the gusts. Outside the fiord it must have been hell. It was in these deadly conditions that the trawlers Ross Cleveland and Notts County approached the entrance to Isafiord. The skipper of Ross Cleveland was Phil Gay, a good fisherman. Although I had never met him personally, I had exchanged fishing reports, and cracked jokes with him over the radio many a time. On the other hand, I knew George Bures, the Notts County's skipper well. We had been friends for years, sailing as deckies together in the Northern Boats, and I had sailed as mate with him in several ships. He was another fine seaman. George's radar was inoperative, probably ice on the scanner, and Phil was doing the piloting with the Cleveland's radar. The men on the ships sheltering in the fiord could make out the two blips on the radar screens about three miles off Aranes Light in the fiord entrance. In normal conditions they would have been safe, but conditions were far from normal. Phil Gay's voice came over the air to the shocked listeners.

"She's going over. Give my love to my wife," and one of the blips vanished from the radar screens. It was as quick as that. A gust of wind had caught the Cleveland and blew her over.

A short time later Notts County sent out a Mayday call. Blind, she had driven ashore.

The Captain of the Icelandic gunboat Odinn called

the ships racing down the fiord to try and help. He knew exactly where Notts County was, and to reach her required local knowledge. He would try to rescue her crew. And he did.

Positioning the gunboat upwind of the stranded vessel the mate, with complete disregard for his own safety, was floated down on a raft. After helping the half-frozen fishermen onto the raft, they were pulled to safety aboard the gunboat. One man had already died of exposure, the mate had an injured leg caused by a block of ice falling on it, and the skipper had frostbitten hands, later having to have fingers amputated. But for the skill and bravery of the Icelanders it could have been a greater tragedy.

Only one man survived from the Ross Cleveland. Harry Eddom, the mate, and two of his shipmates managed to board a liferaft. Wearing his heavy sea gear, Harry was still alive when the raft drove ashore. His companions froze to death. The Icelanders found him, half frozen, next morning in one of the shelters for shipwrecked fishermen which are dotted round Iceland's rugged coast.

The Notts County, 450 tons, was built in 1960 by Goole Shipbuilding Company at a cost of £150,000. She was declared a constructive total loss, and the wreck was bought by an Icelandic business man for £35. She was dragged off the rocks, but as far as I know she never went to sea again. The last time I saw her, her rotting hull formed part of the breakwater in Isafiord harbour, a reminder of the perils that await those men brave, or foolish, enough to face them, and a monument to the courage of all those men who have died trying. Later that year the crew of the Odinn were honoured at a reception held at Grimsby Town Hall, and presented with a silver salver in recognition of their skill and courage. Had that salver been as big as the Town Hall, it would not have been too big.

Subsequent to the dreadful loss of life on the fishing grounds that year, a public outcry, spearheaded by the trawlermen's women, and endured with self-conscious embarrassment by the trawlermen, resulted in a public enquiry into the safety on fishing vessels, and the trawler owners were subjected to the unwelcome glare of the limelight. The findings of the enquiry, the Holland Martin Report, were published, and recommended a number of safety measures, many of them practical, some cosmetic, that should be complied with.

Let's face it. Trawling in the Arctic, or anywhere else for that matter, is a highly dangerous game, and from time to time, loss of life and limb will occur. It is all part of the price to pay for our fish and chips. I have no doubt that many widows on Humberside will insist that the price is too high. In my opinion, the one measure that would have contributed more to safety on the distant water trawlers than all the other recommendations put forward was never considered, or at least, was never implemented.

That measure was to have increased the size of the crews.

When the Icelandic trawler Egill Raudi was lost she carried a crew of 34 men. A British trawler of comparable size, or bigger, doing exactly the same job, under precisely the same conditions, carried a maximum complement of twenty men. In fact, British trawlers carried smaller crews than any of the foreign ships working in the Arctic. The men were called on to work such long hours that when the occasion arose that they had to chop ice off the boat, often they were completely exhausted before they started. Small wonder that the build up of ice beat them so many times. Would you travel on a train if you knew that the driver had been working eighteen hours a day for the past twelve days? Or be happy about flying to Paris knowing that the pilot and navigator had been without sleep for the previous forty-eight hours? How many trawlers have been lost, you may ask, simply because the men in the wheelhouse, senses dulled from want of sleep, failed to react in time to some impending danger.

I can only think of one reason why we were forced to operate the ships with such small crews, and why we were expected to work such outrageous hours. When a ship was lost the underwriter picked up the tab and stood the cost of building a new ship.

The twenty men lost with her were expendable, and could easily be replaced. In economic terms the loss would have no adverse effect on the balance sheet. Financially, the only losers were the widows, who were faced with the problem of raising their children without the help of the main provider. Putting another half dozen deckies aboard the ships would have nibbled away a wee bit of the immense profits that were made, very little of which found its way into the pockets of the men that went through hell to earn them.

According to 'Loss List of Grimsby Fishing Vessels' by David Boswell, between 1919 and 1960, 124 large steam trawlers were lost at sea from one cause or another, excluding the heavy losses sustained

during the 1939-45 war, an average of 3.5 ships a year over the 36 year period. Those figures only refer to ships registered at Grimsby. Include the Hull, Fleetwood, and Aberdeen vessels and the numbers are more than doubled. No statistics exist concerning the number of men lost or crippled, but loss of life and limb must have been enormous. I believe, with hindsight, that it is a disgrace that no system of compensation was ever introduced. The owners did manage a fund, financed by the fishermen themselves, (it was a condition of employment on the trawlers that crew members paid a few pennies a day at sea into this fund: Fishermens Dependant Fund) but the payouts were a pittance. A Fishermens' Pension Scheme was introduced in the 39/45 post war years, contributions being based on the number of days at sea, but the benefits under the scheme were far from generous, and its introduction probably had more to do with relieving the owners of liability under the national pension plan that the fishermens welfare. The retirement pension was paid when the insured man reached the age of 65, and while this is a normal condition in most occupations, the physical demands made by the work on the deck of an Arctic trawler guaranteed that the man able to hold a job down till that age was a very, very rare bird indeed.

The pension scheme was scrapped with the trawlers, and those men that had reached the age of 55 were offered the choice of a lump sum, or a pension when they reached the state retirement age. In my case, the offer was either a lump sum of £190, or a pension of eleven shillings (55p) a week, payment to start ten years in the future. Had I opted for the

pension, at today's prices it would have bought me
one cigarette a day.

Freezing conditions off North Cape, Iceland.

*Deep inside the Artic Circle the trawler begins
to pick up her coating of ice.*

Chapter Fourteen

THE SARGON AND THE HOWE

One of the few pleasures I enjoyed while serving aboard the Arctic trawlers was taking the middle watch, from 11 p.m. till 3 a.m., from the second day on of the homeward passage, when the weather was fine, and there was a good catch stowed down the fishroom. The ship would be quiet save for the throb of her engines, and the hiss of displaced water along her sides.

The seemingly endless hours of toil were over for that trip, and the craving for sleep had been satisfied. Festering cuts, salt water boils, ice burns, and strained muscles had already started to heal, and a fortnight's accumulation of muck, sweat, and fish blood had been washed off our bodies, and with a change of underwear we no longer stank like a herd of polecats.

Miles away from the nearest land and established trade routes, the radar screen devoid of any target, the navigation would be undemanding. A pot of sickly sweet tea would be steaming in the pot rack, the wheelhouse warm and cosy, and with the prospect of ten hours off duty at the end of the watch, and with the delights of a couple of days civilized living looming in the not too distant future, this was the time to get a yarn bent on.

The range of topics we debated during those early morning watches was as wide as the oceans we traversed: the fortunes of Grimsby Town and Hull City football clubs, the chances of the various candidates for the Gold Cup, the merits of the latest female recruits to the port 'meat market', speculation as to the sexual prowess of the female Royals, scandal - both local and in high places, politics, theology, literature, the performing arts. You name it, we gave it a run.

As a young man, too green to make a contribution to this area of folk lore, I used to listen enthralled to the stories of past epics related by my elders. These tales of courage, endurance, or tragedy were always delivered with an absence of sensationalism, and invariably began with "I remember one trip in the...". These tales are legion, I could fill a book. Maybe I will one day, but for now I'll repeat a couple of my favourites, the authenticity of which I have been able to check from contemporary newspapers, or documents supplied by participants or next of kin.

The steam trawler Sargon, 130.2 feet long and 297 tons gross, was built at Beverley in 1913 by Cook, Welton, and Gemmil. On the morning of the 5th January 1923 she sailed from Grimsby under the command of Skipper J. McCarthy, bound for the White Sea grounds, and a place in fishing lore.

Twenty-four hours out of the Humber, in a North

Sea gale, she sighted the distress signals of the trawler Ethel Dutton. A line was secured to the disabled vessel, and the tow towards the shelter offered by the Firth of Forth began. After towing her for over eighty miles the towline had to be cut as the Ethel Dutton sank. Taking the crew off the sinking ship, Sargon proceeded to Leith, where the rescued fishermen were landed together with one of her own crew, Harry Beavers, who had been injured when the tow parted. A replacement deckhand, Johnny Bell, a native of Granton, was signed on and the Sargon set sail.

After a rough passage she arrived off the Murmansk coast and commenced fishing on 20th January, fifteen days after leaving her home port. Fishing was good, and apart from one incident when she was chased by a Russian gunboat, continued uninterrupted. Bound home with a good catch on board, she was reported to have passed the Lofoten Islands on the 3rd February. She should have docked at Grimsby on 7th February, but she never arrived. On the 20th February it was officially announced that all hope had been given up, and Sargon was presumed lost with all hands.

All the functions demanded by etiquette were complied with. The flags on the poles around the fish docks flew at half mast, and the widows wore black. The Padre made his rounds and conducted a service at the bethel. Crew members, long considered a nuisance when ashore, were granted a posthumous moment of glory in the local press. Insurance policies were checked, claims made, paid out, and the money spent. Then the natives of Grimsby, family and friends excepted, began to forget the Sargon and her crew. After all, she was only a trawler, and its loss was not unusual. Many had been lost in the past, and many more would be lost in the future. If you had no one on board, or if any financial interest you had in the vessel was insured, the loss was of little consequence. Only this time the final curtain hadn't fallen.

On 5th February, two days after passing the Lofotens, Sargon ran into hurricane force winds, and was forced to dodge head to wind. Having left for home with barely enough bunkers on board to make the passage, she was soon in trouble. Nets, deck boards, and wood panels were burnt to eke the coal out and keep steam in the boiler. After three days battling against head winds, and making no progress, fuel finally ran out, and she was left to the mercy of wind and tide. The storm abated on 9th February and Sargon found herself drifting helplessly, driven where ever the currents chose to take her.

Food ran out. There was plenty of fish in the hold, and the crew lived on it. Fried until the fat ran out, boiled, and sun dried, but fish won't keep for ever, and as it rotted, seagulls were caught, and unsuccessful attempts were made to catch rats to supplement the diet. Dysentery broke out adding to the men's plight.

On 27th February, as Sargon drifted closer to Iceland, a German trawler, the Schleswig Holstein, spotted her distress signals and came to her assistance. Launching her lifeboat, the crew made two trips to the German trawler to collect much needed stores, and a tow was rigged up. Sargon was towed 200 miles to Reykjavik, where she arrived on 1st March. After taking on coal and provisions she proceeded to Grimsby, via Aberdeen, where she took on more coal. She docked at Grimsby on the evening tide of 10th March after a voyage lasting 65 days.

Word of Sargon's survival had preceded her, and the fishing community gave her a hero's welcome. Every ship in the dock that had steam raised sounded a greeting on its whistle. A huge crowd gathered in Riby Square, but only relatives were allowed access to the Dock Estate. Many touching scenes took place on the quayside as families were united with men that had come back from the dead, although I did hear, but was never able to confirm, that one of the 'widows' had remarried. Nor was I able to discover what action the insurance clubs took over the spent insurance payout.

As the men left the dock they were given a tremendous reception by the crowd waiting in Riby Square, and Skipper McCarthy was chaired shoulder high. Modestly, his only comment was "A greater Captain than I was in command of Sargon."

Due to the hatred of all things German that existed after the Great War, German trawlers were banned from landing their catches at the Humber ports, and moves were afoot to extend the ban to Aberdeen and other Scottish ports. That the crew of Sargon owe their salvation to the efforts and goodwill of their German counterparts again demonstrates the bond of common humanity that exists between men who live on and off the sea, and the code of conduct which unites them, and is stronger than politics when human life is at stake.

The epic voyage of the Sargon had a considerable influence on future trawling practice in that it hastened the fitting of wireless communication equipment on the trawlers, although it was not until well into the thirties that all the ships working the Arctic fishing grounds could boast a radio and direction finder. Today, every distant water trawler is obliged by law to be fitted with radio transmitters with a world wide range, and to carry a qualified wireless operator.

Sargon continued to fish from Grimsby, survived the carnage of World War II, and finally met her end on 1st December 1948 when she was driven ashore at Patreksfjordur, on the west coast of Iceland. Eleven of her seventeen men crew, including her skipper, Albert Edward Jenner, perished in the blizzard with her, but that is another story.

Draw a line on your atlas from North Cape, Norway to South Cape, the southernmost tip of Svalbard (Spitsbergen). Just to the north of the mid point of this line, deep in the Arctic Circle, Latitude 74 degrees 25 minutes north, 19 degrees 5 minutes east, a small island climbs out of the sea. Bjornoya - Bear Island to you - with an area of about 45 square miles, will never become a tourist attraction. Remote, and devoid of human habitation save for the couple of operators manning the wireless station on the north of the island, surrounded by stormy, ice infested waters, it is over 200 miles from the nearest outpost of civilization.

The terrain on the island is as hostile and uninviting as the waters which surround it. Rocky, boulder strewn tracts separate patches of marsh and quicksand. Apart from the low shore of Misery Bay on the eastern side of the island, one of the few spots a landing is feasible, steep craggy cliffs drop down to the water and form a barrier to the storm driven rollers that pound the shoreline. Cape Bull, the southern tip of the island, is particularly steep, and the rocks and reefs that lie close in around its base are always ready to rip the bottom out of any ship foolish enough to stray too close inshore.

For most of the short summer fog and mist shroud the island. The sun never sets, migratory birds arrive, and Arctic fox and rabbit raise their young. They haven't long. By the fall night has started to creep in and the temperature begins to fall. Stunted flora withers and dies back. The fauna either hibernate or don their winter coats. Geese, sea eagle, and snowbirds begin their long trek south in search of warmer climes, and Jack Frost returns to turn the region into a frozen wasteland.

In the perpetual darkness of the polar night life on the land becomes extinct. At sea, seals, walruses and polar bears roam the ice pack, as much at home in the water as on the frozen surface, and the shoals of Arctic cod that feed and breed in the waters of this hostile wilderness attract the trawlermen like a magnet. They gather like moths round a candle. Some of them pay the same price as the moths.

It was at Bear Island, in these wintry conditions, that what must go down in the annals of maritime history as one of the greatest rescues of all time took place. The Grimsby trawler Howe, GY 177, just over a year old, 140 feet long, the latest thing in trawler design, and pride of the fleet, left port on Friday the 13th November 1931, with a crew of fifteen men under the command of Skipper 'Russian' George McGregor. A nor'nor'east course for 540 miles brought Stadland abeam. Steering northeast for a further 330 miles saw Skonvar Light on the south-ern tip of the Lofoten Isles flashing on the starboard beam, and Howe altered course a couple of points to the nor'ard for the 400 miles of the last leg of her passage to Bear Island.

The night of 18th November was wild. Battling through heavy seas, gale force winds, and frequent snow squalls, the ill-fated trawler approached the fishing grounds. An error in the navigation, high wind and sea, and poor visibility all combined, and the result was disaster. At 0345 on the morning of 19th November she touched bottom. In minutes the giant rollers drove her further on to the reef, and she stuck solid. The lights went out as the engine room flooded, and the seas crashed over her, beginning the breaking-up process.

Most of the deck crew were turned in in the fo'c'sle when the vessel stranded, and in pitch darkness, half dressed, they managed to claw their way aft and reach the wheelhouse. There, with the rest of the crew, they passed the dark hours, awaiting the couple of hours twilight that serves as daytime in those northern latitudes. They were to spend the next sixty hours crammed in that small space, in sub zero temperatures, constantly lashed by icy spray, with only a couple of tins of corned beef and some bread to eat. They managed to get some distilled water from the engineroom to drink.

Almost immediately after the stranding, Sam Turner, the wireless operator, was hammering out distress calls, but received no response. In the winter months there are no merchant ships in the area, and in those days the Norwegian coast stations closed down for the night. Not all the trawlers were fitted out with wireless, and aboard those that were the wireless operating duties were regarded as a part time occupation, the operator having to work on deck with the rest of the men during the day. At that early hour they would be snatching a few hours kip, and the radio receivers would be switched off.

At 0700 hours Sam began sending out the distress call again, and was immediately answered by the radio station on the north of the island, who relayed the call to all the fishing vessels within range. The Howe had given her position as being on the west side of Cape Bull, but this was later found to be an error. In fact, she had grounded on the rocks off Bogevika, a little over four miles up the coast. This error is understandable. Electronic navigational aids were still a long way in the future. Echo sounders were just being introduced, and were primitive and unreliable. In a region where poor visibility rules out the use of a sextant for days on end the navigator must fall back on dead reckoning and a pair of good eyes.

Satisfied that trawlers were on their way to the scene of the stranding the two Norwegian operators, Thorlaf Johansen and Egil Lindberg, set off to the reported position of the wreck. Hampered by the darkness, dangerous crevices, and the rough frozen ground, they arrived at Cape Bull, but were unable to locate the stranded vessel. Reluctantly they returned to the wireless station, arriving back late that night, hungry, exhausted and half frozen.

Meantime, aboard the Howe, conditions were deteriorating. Her lifeboats had been smashed and carried away by the seas breaking over her. Her masts were uprooted, and it was evident that her back was broke. Throughout the dark hours Skipper McGregor played the violin to his crew while they constructed a couple of makeshift breeches buoys. These buoys were to prove invaluable later. With the short period of half light that passes for day so far north the shipwrecked men were able to assess their plight. A boiling cauldron of surf about forty yards wide separated them from the foot of the cliffs, and one of the deckhands, George Harmer, was lowered into the raging torrent in an attempt to swim to, and climb the cliff with a line. On his first try George was washed back aboard before he had got more than two yards from the wreck, losing his seaboots in the process. A second attempt also met with failure when, overwhelmed by the heavy surf, he had to be pulled back aboard. The loss of his boots caused him problems later. There was nothing more they could do. If they were to survive help had to come from outside.

Offshore, a score or more trawlers had picked up the distress call relayed by Bear Island Radio, and were battling through heavy seas towards Howe's reported position. On arrival they approached dangerously close to the rocky shore to search for the stranded vessel, finally locating her a few miles north of the Bull, on the sou'west corner of the Island. The rescue vessels grouped on the edge of the deep water. In mountainous seas, an onshore gale, and pitch darkness, there was little they could do other than signal their presence to the shipwrecked men. By next morning, 21st November, weather conditions had improved slightly, and Skipper T. 'Snowy' Worthington tried to take his ship, the Hull trawler Imperialist, close enough to get a line to the wreck, but was forced to back off to deeper water when the ship touched bottom.

Then the Hull trawler Thomas Hardy made an attempt at rescue. Moving in as close as possible she launched her lifeboat. The lifeboat, towing a Carley float, then anchored on the edge of the surf, and Ernie Hunter, deckhand on Thomas Hardy, and George Smith, deckhand on Imperialist, boarded the float and tried to steer it through the breakers to the doomed ship. They managed to get within twenty yards of the wreck when the turbulence among the rocks beat them. Both men were thrown into the sea. George managed to climb back on the float, but Ernie, who had injured his hand, could only hang on to the Carley as it was pulled back to the lifeboat. Attempts were then made to float a line down to the wreck, but the barrel to which the line was fastened was smashed to smithereens on the rocks. It was now obvious to the rescuers that in the prevailing weather conditions rescue from the seaward side was impossible.

While these futile attempts were being made a group of ships which included the Pennine and Cape Spartivento of Hull, and the Elf King of Grimsby, steamed round to the east side of the island and began putting men ashore between Cape Bergesen and Tunheim, close to the wireless station, with the intention of effecting a rescue from the shore side. The problems they had to surmount were frightening. Nine miles of frozen boulder strewn terrain had to be crossed, double that distance when necessary detours were taken into account. Deep crevices, quicksand, and meres had to be got round, and there was only about two hours twilight to use. Due to ore deposits compasses were useless, and there was always the chance of meeting a hungry polar bear. If that wasn't enough they had to contend with subzero temperatures, and a raging blizzard. Finally, there would be the job of somehow getting fifteen exhausted men up an almost sheer two hundred foot cliff face, and escorting them back across the island.

A number of parties set out to cross the island and locate the wreck. In their eagerness to get going the initial parties were ill-equipped for the task. Some got lost, and after walking in circles, had to start again. Others found the going too tough, and exhaustion and frostbite forced them to give up. The third or fourth party to make the attempt was led by Skipper E. Drinkall of the Elf King, and included Francis Frith, Bill Coulbeck, Harry Osborne, Johnny Walton, George Burrel, Bob Glentworth, Lester Brooks, and Tom Giles. The Norwegian wireless operator, Johansen, joined this party as a guide.

At 0700 hours, carrying lights, ropes, and a supply of food the party began their march. It was not long before the harsh climate, and the hostile nature of the terrain started to take its toll. Some of the men were unable to keep pace with the leaders and began to drop back. The vanguard, comprised of Skipper Drinkall, deckhand Bill Coulbeck of Elf King, third hand George Burrel of Cape Spartivento, and the Norwegian operator pressed on. They all knew that speed was vital. It would not take long for the sea to pound the Howe to bits. Once that happened it would be curtains for the men they were striving to save.

Striking the coast above the position of the wreck, they made their way southward along the cliff top, probably guided by the lights of the trawlers lying offshore. Shortly before 1400 hours, Saturday 21st November, they located the wreck at the foot of the cliffs. The trek across the island had taken them seven hours.

Aboard the Howe the men were miserable, cold, wet, tired, and hungry. They had been stranded on the rocks and confined to the wheelhouse for 58 hours. The generator was under water, and the batteries that powered their wireless transmitter were flat, hence they had no communication with the world beyond the surf one side, and the cliffs on the other. They were ignorant of the progress of efforts, if any, that were being made to help them, and their ship was beginning to disintegrate from the constant pounding of the sea. They knew their future lifespan could be measured in hours, rather than days. If help was to come, it had to come quickly. There wasn't much time left. Imagine their joy on seeing the lights on the cliff top.

George Burrel was lowered down the 200 foot precipice and managed to float a line out to the wreck. Taking the line aboard, the shipwrecked fishermen rigged their home made breeches buoy as quickly as frozen fingers would allow. The first man to leave the stricken ship and be hauled up the cliff face was the 16 year old apprentice, Charlie Major. Initially, the job of pulling the men up the cliff was slow, hard graft, but the rescuers that had been left behind rejoined the team, and with their weight on the rope, the process speeded up. The first of the makeshift buoys broke, but was quickly replaced with the second one. The last man to be dragged off the doomed trawler was her skipper, Russian George, a giant of a man. As soon as George's feet touched

terra firma Johansen flashed a morse message to the trawlers lying just offshore "All the men have been got ashore."

Whistles blew, and those ships with wireless spread the good news. Sheer guts and determination had brought off the greatest sea rescue of all time, against almost impossible odds. Grace Darling would have applauded these men.

But the survivor's ordeal was not over yet. They were ill clad to battle against the cold of the Arctic night. Most of them were poorly shod. Harmer, the man who had lost his boots in the attempt to swim ashore, had his feet wrapped in wads of newspaper bound in place with hessian sacking. Rescuers and rescued were feeling the effects of frostbite, and there was twenty miles of rugged, frozen terrain to cross.

They set off on their trek. Progress was slow, Mr. Harmer having to be half-carried. Then they met up with another party heading for the scene of the wreck. This party was extremely well equipped, and lighting a fire under the lee of a large boulder, a ships tin of toddy was hotted up, and cheese and corned beef sandwiches devoured. One of the newcomers gave up his boots to Mr Harmer and wrapped his own feet in the discarded sack cloth.

Having ate and drank, they got under way again, Harmer having to be carried on an improvised stretcher for the last part of the journey. They eventually reached the other side of the island at 0930 hours the next morning. It had taken Skipper Drinkall and his men twenty-six hours to complete the round trip.

The survivors were first taken to the wireless station where the wives of the operators had prepared them a hot meal, then they were escorted to the Elf King for the passage to Tromso, Norway. At Tromso half of them were transferred to the Hull trawler Danesman and both ships headed for Grimsby and home.

Though the rescue had been successful beyond wildest dreams there was a price to pay. Most of the survivors, and some of the rescuers, suffered from severe frostbite, and George Harmer, his nerves shattered by the experience, never went to sea again.

Back in the U.K. news of the rescue received wide acclaim, and details of the drama were blazoned across the pages of the national press. The following is an extract from a report that appeared in one newspaper:

HEROES OF THE SEA - HULL AND GRIMSBY MEN

The King has been pleased (says a Board of Trade Announcement) to award the Bronze Medal For Gallantry in saving life at sea to:

George Harmer, deckhand on the steam trawler Howe of Grimsby.

Ernest Hunter, deckhand on the trawler *Thomas Hardy* of Hull

George W Smith deckhand on the trawler Imperialist of Hull.

In addition the Board of Trade have awarded:

Pieces of silver plate to T. Johansen and E. Lindberg, wireless operators, Bear Island, and to Skipper E. Drinkall of the trawler *Elf King* of Grimsby. Also a binocular glass to Skipper T. Worthington of the trawler *Imperialist* of Hull.

Other inscribed souvenirs (silver cigarette cases) to Francis Frith, Ist Engineman, William Mantrip, 2nd Hand, Henry Walker, deckhand, William Coulbeck and Frank Crawford, trimmers, and Frederic Thornton, deckhand-fireman all of the *Elf King* Grimsby. To Robert Milliner, 2nd hand, George Burrel, 3rd hand, Charles Wallace, boatswain, Robert Glentworth, cook, and Lester Brooks, Thomas Giles, and Thomas Hodgson, spare hands on *Cape Spartivento* of Hull. and to Harold Hobson, 2nd hand, Walter Ruinsey, 3rd hand, William Hatton, boatswain, and Arthur Rogers and John Walton, spare hands of the *Pennine* of Hull.

These awards have been granted in recognition of services rendered in connection with the rescue of the crew of the steam trawler *Howe* of Grimsby.

The *Sargon* saga had indicated the need for wireless equipment to be installed on trawlers. In the case of the *Howe* it is probable that without the 1/4 kilowatt Marconi spark transmitters she, and other ships in the vicinity, were fitted, her plight would not have been noticed, and her name would have been added to the long list of trawlers and crews that have vanished without trace. In the event, the wireless operators on *Elf King, Imperialist, Cape Spartivento*, and *Pennine* kept a continuous watch for the entire 72 hours of the rescue operation, and provided the vital link with the parties involved. Their dedication was rewarded with an award from the Hull and Grimsby Trawler Owners' Insurance Company some months later. At the same time presentations were made to Skippers T. Turner and J. Dahlgreen of *Cape Spartivento* and *Pennine*.

An unconfirmed report stated that Howe completely broke up three hours after her crew were taken off, and two independent sources have told me that there was no trace of the wreck two days later.

Fifty years on, in an article in the Grimsby Evening Telegraph, Steve Richards stated:

"...one good thing appears to have come out of the disaster. It seems that the incident led to some sort of a marker being placed on Bear Island to alert other trawlers fishing those rich but deadly fishing grounds."

If that were the case, I've never seen it, and I made several trips to the waters round Bear Island in every year between 1947 and 1968.

Subsequently, at the Board of Trade enquiry into the loss, Skipper McGregor was cleared of any negligence leading up to the stranding, and continued to fish the Arctic grounds until his sudden death in 1945.

Charlie Major, *Howe's* young apprentice continued to follow a fishing career eventually becoming a successful skipper with the Butt Group. Another member of the *Howe's* crew, Ernie Lovat, also became a well known skipper, and was fishing until he retired in the early seventies.

George Burrel, who played such an important part in the rescue, was another of the men involved who became skippers. After commanding a minesweeper throughout World War II, Skipper Lieutenant Burrel returned to fishing with the Lord Line. He retired from the sea at the age of 52 to run the grocery business he had bought. I am indebted to his widow for much of the detail concerning the loss of the *Howe*.

Howe wasn't the only loss suffered by the Grims-by distant water fleet that month. On the 2nd the Offa foundered off the Norwegian coast, and on the 15th the *Frida Sophia* stranded on Vestmanaejar, Iceland and was a total loss.

Seven years after the *Howe* epic trawlermen were again called on to trek across Bear Island on a mercy mission. On Friday, 30th September 1938 the Hull trawler St. Sebastian pulled the gear aboard in foul weather northeast of Bear Island and set course for home. Shortly afterwards she grounded on rocks off the north coast of the island. Four Hull trawlers, *Davy, Cape Duner, Mildenhall,* and *Loch Oskaig,* and the Norwegian salvage vessel *Jason* picked up her distress call and were quickly on the scene, but as in the case of the HOWE stranding, the weather was too severe to allow them to make physical contact with the wreck. The *Loch Oskaig* reported that only the *St. Sebastian's* mast and funnel were visible above water, but that a man was seen climbing over the rocks. *The Davy* and *Cape Duner* immediately steamed round to Tunheim and put a ten man landing party ashore. Assisted by the operators from the wireless station they combed the cliffs along the north coast. The search was in vain. There were no survivors. On Sunday 2nd October, the weather had moderated sufficiently to allow the skipper of *The Davy,* and the captain of the *Jason* to board the wreck at low tide. They found two corpses in the wheelhouse. Another ship and crew were added to the long list of those that had made a one-way trip to the Arctic fishing grounds.

Stormy weather.

Chapter Fifteen

THE END OF THE LINE

My departure from the Humber fishing scene was unpremeditated and unexpected. One of my failings, not my only one I might add, has always been an unerring ability to say the wrong thing, at the wrong time, to the wrong person. As my wife puts it, I am inclined to open my mouth and let the wind blow my tongue about. That talent led to me saying goodbye to Grimsby Fish Dock and discovering that there are less strenuous ways of earning a living.

I was sailing as mate with Skipper Barry Jacklin in one of the Ross Group's distant water trawlers at the time. Barry was stopping off for a holiday that trip, and as I had been with him for some time I expected, as was customary, to be taking the ship away while he was off. After our fish was sold, and my other jobs seen to, I went home for breakfast. On returning to the office to draw my pay I received the news that Mr. Hudson wanted to see me. The Ross Group had just taken over the Hudson Trawling Company, and in the management reorganization Mr. Hudson had moved from Hull to take charge of the Grimsby office.

I climbed the stairs to his office confident that I would be going skipper of the ship for the two trips. Not so.

"Your skipper is stopping off for the next couple of trips, Nicklin," he told me. "I think this is the time of the year to take a young man straight from the nautical school and give him a chance." That was a kick in the teeth. I didn't like it, and the wind got to work on my tongue.

"At the same time you can get another young man straight from school to go mate with him. I'll take my holiday." I replied.

That wasn't what he had in mind. "If you stop off there is no guarantee you'll get your job back," he leaned on me.

I wasn't in the mood to be leaned on.

"You can stuff the ship up your arse, and all the other Ross boats after her if there's room, Mr. Hudson. Good day."

I stalked downstairs to the runner's office, signed off the ship, and was half way down Fishdock Road before I began to regret my impetuosity. I fully expected to be unemployed for some time, but the offer of a job from an unexpected quarter rescued me from my self-inflicted predicament.

A Mr. David Milligan phoned me. He was, he said, Marine Superintendent for the Ghana State Fishing Corporation. The Corporation had two factory freezer trawlers under construction at Newport Shipbuilding Company's yard at Newport, Mon. Was I interested in joining one of them as Chief Mate, and working from Tema, Ghana on a contract basis. On learning I was more than interested he came round to see me to discuss the job.

I was offered an initial contract for one year with a basic salary of £3,000 per annum, plus 18 shillings per ton of fish caught, subject to Ghanaian income tax. I would be paid £60 gear allowance, and receive 60 days U.K. leave on full pay each year.

One Monday afternoon, three weeks later, I arrived in Newport to take up my new post. I spent the next three years fishing from Tema.

I arrived back in Grimsby to find that the high price of oil was driving those trawling companies operating the near and middle water trawlers to the wall. Their ships were being laid up, sold to foreign interests, or scrapped, and family concerns which had been in business since the turn of the century were putting the shutters up.

In Iceland the Cod War was reaching its final stages, and a blind man could see that the distant water trawling industry was in terminal decline. Trawlers were going to be laid up on a massive scale, and before very long over 5,000 trawlermen were going to be scrambling for the limited number of sea-going jobs that were available. Jobs on the distant water trawlers were becoming as scarce as hen's teeth.

From a personal viewpoint I had learned two lessons during my time with the State Fishing Corporation. First, there are more friendly environments to work in than the Arctic Seas, and second, it is possible to earn a good living without having to swill about the deck for eighteen hours a day.

During my sojourn in Ghana I had put on three stone in weight, and my hands, once as hard as paving slabs, were now as soft as a baby's bottom. Even had the prospects for Arctic trawling looked more rosy I doubt if I would have been prepared to accept the rigours of the life again. In the event, after a disastrous business venture in inshore fishing, a contact I had made in Tema offered me a job as Chief Mate on an American flag supply boat working from Port Gentil in the Gabon.

The pay was 40 dollars a day tax free, good money at the time, and I accepted the job with alacrity. Two days later I was on a plane to Libreville to join the *Caspian Seahorse*. For a couple of months we were fetching and carrying for a drilling rig about twenty miles offshore, then we moved to Pointe Noire in the Congo. After a spell working from that port I paid off, I spent the next twelve years until my retirement working as Chief Officer on hydrographic survey vessels. This was the sort of job trawlermen dreamed about, never really believing such jobs existed. Eight weeks on board followed by a month at home. Two four hour watches a day, and no survey work if the wind got above force 5 or 6. Half the winter spent tied up to the quay or anchored in a sheltered cove. First Class travel to and from ship, excellent feeding, a zero stress factor, and a respectable salary cheque at the end of every month. A far cry from Arctic trawling, but it was the expertise learned on the turbulent fishing grounds that enabled the trawler skipper to handle this type of work so competently.

A lot has been said about the plight of the thousands of men thrown on the scrap heap when the trawlers were scrapped. In reality, the skippers and mates were, in the main, able to find alternative employment. You will find them scattered all over the seven seas. Driving coasters up and down the North Sea, on the dredgers scooping up gravel instead of fish, on the diving support and oilrig service vessels, and sailing as skipper and mate on the Spanish 'quota hoppers'. Some have moved away as far as Australia, New Zealand and the Falkland Islands to continue trawling.

It is the majority of the men, those deck rats with no written qualifications to prove their competence, that require assistance. They are not seeking charity. They never will. For years, many of them worked for the same company. They paid National Insurance contributions, and contributed to the Redundancy Fund. By any moral standards you care to apply, these men are entitled to redundancy pay. Most of them are in their twilight years, and may not see the end of their fight for justice against the inadequacies of the employment legislation. In the interests of decency and fair play the Government should stop dragging its feet, and pay these men compensation for their loss.

Apart from the breaking up of local communities, I predict that one day the disbandment of this unique breed of men will be a serious loss to the nation. In two world wars, each one widely proclaimed to be the war to end wars, the trawlermen and their ships took on the highly dangerous job of sweeping the sea lanes free of mines. It cost many of them their lives, but the value to the war effort of the countless merchant seamen, and numerous ships and cargoes, who owe their survival to the way the 'sweepers performed their task is incalculable.

Throughout the uneasy peace between the wars the trawlermen went about their business of bringing home food for the nation, at the same time attuning themselves to Mother Nature and her violent moods. When hostilities broke out they were there. A legion of expert seamen, accustomed to flirting with danger, trained at no cost to the public purse, and ready to don uniform and swap their quarry from fish to mines and submarines. They could be ready for active service in less time than it took the shipyards to equip their boats with the paravanes, asdic, depth charges, guns and other bits and pieces needed for their new role.

If history repeats itself, and it makes a habit of doing just that, sometime in the future there will be another global confrontation, and this island of ours will again be threatened. The cargoes we rely on for survival will come by sea, and the high tech boys will develop more ingenious explosive devices designed to destroy the ships and men that carry those cargoes. Now that the trawlers have been scrapped, and the breed of men that manned them are an endangered species, where will the hundreds of ships, and the thousands of men to man them, come from.

Ships can be built, and men can be trained, you say. Yes, a land lubber can be taught the rudiments of navigation in a classroom in a few weeks, but it takes a lot longer, in a harsher environment, to learn to live with the sea in all its moods. And, in the event of hostilities breaking out, that time will not be available. Then the trawlermen will be sadly missed.

I have been asked more than once if I ever regretted making distant water fishing a career. I don't regret one minute of it, but if asked whether, starting out again, would I follow the same road, the answer would be, in all honesty, I don't know. When I first started out I had little conception of the hardship and danger that went hand in hand with the job, and being brought up in a community where going to sea was the normal way of life, I accepted my lot as standard.

Now that I am older, possibly wiser, and am fully aware of all aspects of the life, I doubt if I would have the guts to go through it again.

Sometimes in the early hours, when the wind is moaning though the branches of the apple trees at the bottom of my garden, my mind goes back in time. I recall the violence of the storm that took Lorella and Roderigo, I relive the afternoon when Thuringia almost capsized, I see the faces of the many friends and shipmates who perished, frozen and alone, in those icy wastes. Then, further sleep impossible, I creep downstairs and make a cuppa.

But there were more pleasant times. Trips when the weather was kind, fish was plentiful, we hit the right market, had a good pay day, and concluded the voyage with a glorious piss-up.

I believe that, for the most part, that what a man does is what a man is, and whatever sort of man I am was moulded on the deck and bridge of a trawler. These days, in the more genteel surroundings of the local bridge club where I spend most of my leisure evenings, if asked what I did for a living, I always reply that I was once a trawlerman. I am proud I was once one of them, and I'm glad I went. In their fight for redundancy pay I wish them well. God knows, they deserve it.

A Royal Navy warship and an Icelandic gunboat jockey for position during a 'Cod War' encounter.

The Icelandic Cod Wars. Bumps-a-daisy. A Royal Navy ship heads off an Icelandic gunboat trying to cut away a trawler's gear.
The cutting gear is clearly visible leading from the gunboat's stern.